Portrait in Oil

Portrait in Oil

An Illustrated History of BP

Berry Ritchie

JAMES X JAMES

Acknowledgements

The author would like to thank Rodney Chase and Robert Pennant Jones for making this book possible, Peter Brigg and Valerie Shepard for their unstinting editorial and project management efforts, and Sir David Simon, Sir Peter Walters and Sir David Steel for their first-hand contributions to his understanding of BP's recent history.

An illustrated history such as this depends heavily on the quality of its pictorial material. Here the support of Colin Underhill, Margaret Humphrey and Lesley Ubee in BP's photographic library, and of Jane Dobson, Michael Gasson, Anita Hollier and Valerie Johnson at BP's archive at Warwick University, was indispensable.

The author is also indebted to Dr Ronald Ferrier, whose first volume of BP's history was a rich source of material.

Above all, he wishes to express his gratitude to Dr James Bamberg, BP's official historian and the author of volume two of *The History of the British Petroleum Company*, who shared his profound knowledge of the company so generously.

Copyright © 1995
The British Petroleum
Company p.l.c.
Britannic House
1 Finsbury Circus
London EC2M 7BA
United Kingdom

First published 1995

ISBN 0 907383 67X

Designed by
John Rice
Bartlett Rice Associates

Printed and bound by
Butler & Tanner Limited

Published by
James & James
(Publishers) Limited
Gordon House Business Centre
6 Lissenden Gardens
London NW5 1LX
United Kingdom

Picture acknowledgements

Art Directors' Photo Library
72; 79 (margin bottom);
Camera Press Ltd 26 (inset),
28 (top), 90 (in text), 91, 113
(margin top), 117 (margin
top); Daily Express 77 (in text),
126 (margin top); Hulton
Deutsch Collection Ltd 57
(inset), 60 (top and bottom),
62, 65, 68 (margin), 74
(margin), 78 (top), 79 (top),
87, 88 (margin top), 90
(margin), 99 (margin top),
120 (margin); J. Allan Cash
Ltd 8, 24 (margin bottom); The
Illustrated London News
Picture Library 32; Imperial
War Museum 26-7, 28
(bottom), 30 (margin), 56, 64
(top); Robert Harding Picture
Library 13 (margin top), 18, 22
(margin top), 38 (margin), 44.

All other pictures were
supplied either by BP's
photographic library or by BP's
archive at Warwick University.

Contents

Front cover picture
Supply ship approaches
BP's Forties Bravo platform
in the North Sea. Oil
painting by Ben Maile, 1975.

Half-title page
BP advertisement, 1928.

Facing title page
BP service station, 1995.

Facing introduction
British Petroleum Company
share certificate, 1917.

Endpapers
Seismic trace, onshore
oilfield.

The story of BP is multi-layered.

It is an adventure story, beginning with a dramatic search for oil in Persia which led to the development of the entire Middle East, and moving on to equally exciting discoveries in North Africa, the North Sea and North America.

It is a tale of human genius and endeavour, of the development of whole new industries to exploit the hidden wealth of the globe in unbelievably harsh and challenging circumstances.

It is a political drama, rich in intrigue, with BP's fate inextricably entwined in the endless struggle between nations for control of one of the world's most valuable resources.

It is also an illustration of the development of society in a century in which almost every aspect of life, from the motor car to the plastic bag, has become dependent on oil products.

But above all it is the story of the evolution of a company. BP's history began as a gamble by a single entrepreneur. It has grown into a world-wide organization, making a vital contribution to modern society.

This is necessarily a brief account and much has had to be left out or given only a passing reference. There is room for mention of just a few of the many people responsible for the company's survival and growth. The story of BP reveals how men and women working together can build an organization that survives and prospers through the years, however testing the circumstances.

My dictionary describes a company as a number of persons associated together by interests or for carrying on business. But it first defines a company as a society, a companionship, a fellowship.

By any definition, BP is a great company.

Berry Ritchie

Chapter One

The Persian Concession

Left Zagros mountains, near Shiraz, Persia.

The story of the giant multinational oil company that is today called British Petroleum begins, formally at least, on 28 May 1901, when His Imperial Majesty Muzaffar al-Din Shah signed a concession granting William Knox D'Arcy 'a special and exclusive privilege to search for, obtain, exploit, develop, render suitable for trade, carry away and sell natural gas, petroleum, asphalt and ozokerite . . . for a term of sixty years'. The concession covered all of Persia except the five northern provinces.

The Shah's motive for granting this vast concession was money. In 1900 the once-mighty Persian Empire was in a state of economic torpor and financial impoverishment. Total government revenues were only about £1.3m. and the almost powerless Shah was in constant financial difficulty. The concession gave his government £20,000 sterling 'in cash' within one month of the formation of the first company to exploit any oil discovery, as well as £20,000 in shares and a promise of 16 per cent of net profits.

Right Shooting-party at William Knox D'Arcy's country house in Norfolk, 1897. D'Arcy is third from the right.

William D'Arcy's motive was also money, but in his case the desire to make more. He was already very wealthy. Just over 50, he had made a fortune in Queensland, Australia, from the Mount Morgan gold-mining company, which he had helped finance in 1886. By 1900 D'Arcy had returned to England as chairman of Mount Morgan's London board, with a town house in Grosvenor Square, a country mansion at Stanmore in Middlesex and a shoot in Norfolk. Generous and hospitable, he led the self-indulgent life of a rich gentleman. He had not, however, lost interest in making money and he continued to invest in interesting ventures.

William Knox D'Arcy, the man who started it all. His passion for oil nearly lost him his fortune but he died a rich man in 1917. He never set foot in Persia.

D'Arcy had been introduced to the idea of looking for oil in Persia by a friend, the Earl of Orford. Orford, in turn, had been approached by his uncle, Sir Henry Drummond Wolff, who had been the British Minister in Tehran in the late 1880s. There he had got to know General Antoine Kitabgi, a close friend of the Persian Prime Minister, Amin al-Sultan. It was Kitabgi who had asked Wolff, at a meeting in Paris in October 1900, whether he knew an English capitalist who might be interested in acquiring a concession.

D'Arcy proved very interested. He was particularly impressed by a report of exciting oil prospects in Persia written in 1890 by a French geologist named, appealingly to him, Jacques de Morgan.

It turned out that de Morgan was indirectly involved in the proposal Wolff put to D'Arcy. This strengthened D'Arcy's enthusiasm, although he took the precaution of discussing it with Dr Boverton Redwood, Britain's leading oil consultant, before deciding that the gamble was worth taking.

Then he dispatched Alfred Marriott, a level-headed young cousin of one of his investment advisers, to Tehran with full powers to negotiate the concession. By the standards of the Persian court, Marriott achieved this remarkably quickly, as he arrived in Tehran only five weeks before the concession was signed. The negotiations were, however, strongly influenced by Russian objections. D'Arcy countered these with promises of generous

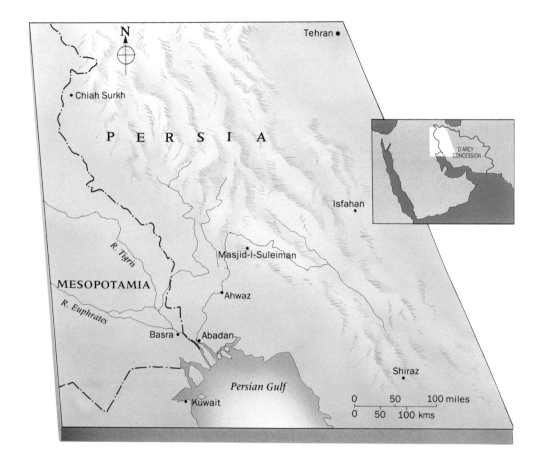

Facing page The concession agreement, signed by His Imperial Majesty Muzaffar al-Din Shah in 1901, granted D'Arcy the exclusive right to extract and sell oil and natural gas from the whole of Persia, excluding the five northern provinces.

Map of south-west Persia showing early oil exploration sites. Drilling began at Chiah Surkh in 1902. The inset map shows the whole area of the concession granted to D'Arcy.

investment in Persia which, fortunately, did not need to be fulfilled. But he did have to provide Kitabgi with £10,000 in cash to help the general 'arrange matters' with the Prime Minister and other influential politicians.

Signing the concession did not, in fact, provide the Shah himself with ready money, as the first official payment of £20,000 fell due only on the formation of a company to exploit any discovery. But as that had to take place within two years, D'Arcy did not have long to find out if de Morgan's optimism about Persia's oil prospects was well founded.

Aware of the need for a quick strike, D'Arcy had already sent one of Redwood's geologists, H T Burls, off to Persia early in 1901 to survey the various places where de Morgan had found signs of oil. By the time the concession was signed, Burls had examined two areas 300 miles apart. The more promising was called Chiah Surkh, about 350 miles west of Tehran and roughly the same distance north of the Persian Gulf. Burls reported to Redwood on 30 July: 'Petroleum undoubtedly occurs in the region under highly favourable geological conditions. The conditions are obviously such as to afford ample justification for the expenditure necessary to prove the commercial value of the interests acquired and it appears . . . only reasonable to assume that the outcome of the work will be the creation of a highly profitable industry of great magnitude.'

Armed with this optimistic assessment, an engineer named George Reynolds was given a one-year contract at a salary of £1,500 to take charge of the exploration programme. A spare, taciturn loner in his late forties, Reynolds had qualified at the Royal Indian Engineering College and been employed in the Indian Public Works Department before working for Royal Dutch in the Sumatran oilfields. Tough, hard-working and self-reliant, he was a competent if mostly self-trained geologist. Just as importantly, he was a natural linguist and a good horseman with a talent for getting things done.

Reynolds reached Tehran in September and spent ten days listening to – but not always taking – advice from Kitabgi before leaving for Chiah Surkh, which he reached at the end of October. A fortnight later he was in Baghdad, which was only 125 miles south-west of the oil prospect. Soon after he was in Basra, the port at the head of the Persian Gulf, unloading the first plant and machinery shipped from the UK.

A slow trek across the Mesopotamian plains to the mountainous valleys in the north began in spite of a shortage of mules, makeshift wagons and obstructions from Turkish officials. Reynolds also had to win over the leader of the Kurdish tribe which occupied the region surrounding Chiah Surkh. 'The authority of the Shah was held in low esteem by our host,' he reported drily, and the landowners 'had no idea of the mineral rights of the owner of the land being nil' but 'required payment over and above that laid down in the concession'.

It was not until November 1902 that drilling began on a small plateau in the mountains with a stream near by. Reynolds had six Polish and

George Reynolds (left) at lunch, Persia, 1910.

Reynolds had to negotiate with local tribal leaders such as Aziz Khan and Muhammed Karim Khan before any work could begin at Chiah Surkh.

Canadian drillers, three or four machinists, two blacksmiths from central Europe, a few rigmen, including some from the Azerbaijani oilfields at Baku, an Indian doctor, a Turkish surveyor, two English assistants, various cooks, firemen and servants, and a fearsome collection of Persian and Kurdish guards to keep off the local tribesmen.

The water was foul, the insects were vicious and there were constant

Left By 1900 the Baku oilfields in Azerbaijan were extensively developed. They were known as the Eternal Fires. Reynolds recruited rigmen from Baku to work in Persia.

Below Typical landscape in the region of Shiraz in south-west Persia.

interruptions owing to bad weather, breakages, sickness and religious festivals. Reynolds coped with everything, conciliatory and firm in turn, soon speaking fluent if ungrammatical Persian and Kurdish, and winning the respect of the local tribes. He was less popular with Kitabgi's minion, the Sheikh al-Mulk, who complained constantly of the Englishman's 'avarice', by which he meant his refusal to let the Persian ingratiate himself with local dignitaries by handing out gifts.

In spite of the delays, the first well was down to 900 ft by the time Reynolds, whose contract had expired, left for England in February 1903, leaving a young American engineer called Rosenplaenter in his place. He knew he was returning to a very anxious employer. Only two months remained before D'Arcy must form a company and pay the Shah £20,000 or lose the concession. When Reynolds arrived in England he found D'Arcy had received a cable from Rosenplaenter on 22 March reporting encouraging indications of oil. The news was enough to persuade D'Arcy to form the First Exploitation Company with a capital of £600,000 in £1 shares on 21 May 1903. The Persian government was sent its money and shareholding, Kitabgi and Wolff were rewarded with small stakes, and D'Arcy issued himself with 350,000 shares in return for his efforts and expenditure so far – which was far, far more than he had expected to invest without a definite return in sight.

By the middle of 1903, in truth, D'Arcy's finances were becoming dangerously stretched. He was under particular pressure from Lloyds Bank to do something about his overdraft, which had risen to £150,000. Clearly, he needed to find new sources of capital to fund the oil search, especially as he was facing Persian demands to begin exploration in areas further south, as well as continuing the drilling at Chiah Surkh.

One possible source of finance was the British Admiralty. The Navy had begun experimenting with oil as fuel in 1898 and an oil fuel

Below Reynolds' first well – Chiah Surkh, started in 1902.

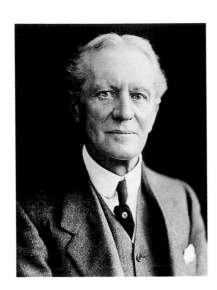

Sir Boverton Redwood, the leading petroleum expert of his day, consultant to the Admiralty and the Burmah Oil Company.

committee had been set up late in 1902 under the auspices of Admiral Sir John Fisher to examine the availability of oil supplies, with a particular brief to bring these under British control. One of its members was Boverton Redwood.

Fisher, who became First Sea Lord in 1903, was an outspoken advocate of using oil instead of coal as fuel for Britain's warships. By luck or judgement, D'Arcy met Fisher in July at Carlsbad, where they were both taking a cure for the usual complaints suffered by over-large Edwardian gentlemen. The Admiral expressed great interest in D'Arcy's Persian venture and promised it his support.

D'Arcy wrote to Ernest Pretyman, president of the Admiralty Oil Committee, asking for a loan. Pretyman told him to try Lord Selborne, the First Lord of the Admiralty, who said 'No'. He received a more encouraging response from Lord Lansdowne, the Foreign Secretary, who wrote to Lord Curzon, the Viceroy of India, that he worried about Persia's oil falling under Russian control if D'Arcy was unable to finance his exploration programme. Curzon, who had been a director of the just-wound-up Persian Bank Mining Rights Corporation, which had had its own ill-fated concession in the 1890s, was dismissive.

D'Arcy pledged more of his Mount Morgan shares against his growing overdraft and tried the Rothschilds. Late in February 1904 he met Alphonse Rothschild in Cannes and told him that the second well at Chiah Surkh had produced 600 barrels of oil in 24 hours six weeks earlier. He did not stress that this flow had tailed off rapidly. Rothschilds decided that the deal they had already reached with Royal Dutch-Shell six months earlier was more attractive.

In near desperation, D'Arcy approached Standard Oil, but these talks, too, petered out. On 19 May, D'Arcy instructed George Reynolds, who had been rehired the previous October to conduct the southern search, not to make any fresh contracts. On 8 June, D'Arcy ordered Reynolds to return to England. On 23 June, all operations were suspended at Chiah Surkh.

Then Boverton Redwood introduced D'Arcy to Burmah Oil.

Burmah Oil had been founded in 1886 by a group of Scotsmen led by David Cargill. Run from offices in Glasgow and London, its main operations were in Burma, where by 1904 Burmah Oil was producing 4,000 barrels a day of high-quality oil. With assets valued at more than £2.5m., Burmah Oil was the second largest British oil company after Shell. In July 1904 Cargill's son John, Burmah Oil's new chairman, was coincidentally finalizing a contract to supply the Admiralty with 350,000 barrels of fuel oil a year. As Cargill admitted to the ubiquitous Redwood, who had been Burmah Oil's consultant since he had sold it a refining patent in 1890, his company's own exploration programme was not going well and there were serious worries about its long-term reserves. The attractions of a major Persian discovery were obvious.

Cargill and his deputy, Charles Wallace, met William D'Arcy for the first time on 10 August 1904. By the end of November agreement had been reached for a new company called the Concessions Syndicate to take over from the First Exploitation Company. The new syndicate undertook to spend up to £70,000 in the following three years on drilling for oil in the south and to give D'Arcy £25,000 towards the £225,000 he reckoned he had spent in Persia so far. If no oil was found, D'Arcy had to pay back the £25,000 and the agreement would end.

If oil was found in commercial quantities, however, a new company would be formed which would raise new capital to repay D'Arcy his outstanding £200,000 and finance the development of the discovery. D'Arcy had trouble selling the deal to Wolff and Vincent Kitabgi, who had inherited the general's minority holding in the First Exploitation Company on his father's death two years earlier. On 5 May 1905 the Concessions Syndicate was finally incorporated with a capital of £100,000 and the 84-year-old Lord Strathcona, one of Britain's wealthiest men, as its figurehead chairman.

As well as raising new capital, the Concessions Syndicate also brought new management to the search for oil in Persia. D'Arcy had been carrying the main burden of responsibility at the London end, assisted only by his secretary and one or two staff of the Mount Morgan mining company in London. The Concessions Syndicate brought the management of the Persian venture under the wing of Burmah Oil. The Syndicate's chairman was John Cargill and its directors included Robert Adamson and James Hamilton, both from Burmah Oil.

George Reynolds set out for Persia to begin the search anew. This time he was going to try drilling at Shardin, one of the two areas prospected the previous year when it was becoming obvious that Chiah Surkh was not going to be viable. Shardin was near the town of Ramhormoz, only 100 miles north-east of Basra. There was even a road to Shardin, unlike the other prospect, the Maidan-i-Naftun near Masjid-i-Suleiman (Solomon's Mosque), about 50 miles further north.

Before the Concessions Syndicate could begin drilling, however, it had to obtain the support of the local tribe, the Bakhtiari. It was not until 16 October that Reynolds and the British Consul-General in Isfahan finally managed to meet the four most influential Bakhtiari khans (chiefs) and it took a month to obtain permission to search for oil on their lands. The key to the five-year deal was an annual fee of £2,000, ostensibly to pay for local guards to protect the syndicate's operations. It was a disastrous arrangement, as the fee was payable to the khans, who never passed on any cash. So none of the money ever reached the guards themselves, with the result that they were as much a threat as a safeguard. Reynolds was far from satisfied with the bargain.

But at least he was finally able to visit Shardin for the first time and plan his drilling programme. Getting it started was a different matter. It took ten days for the first caravan of carts loaded with plant and machinery to struggle the 70 miles from Ahwaz to Shardin. Only by using boiler smokestacks as impromptu water tunnels could many of the larger irrigation canals be crossed.

It was eight months before drilling began and even then Reynolds

Lord Strathcona, chairman of the Concessions Syndicate, which was established with Burmah Oil in 1905. He was later chairman of Anglo-Persian from 1909 to 1914.

15

Bakhtiari guards.

The boiler of Well No. 1 has been preserved at Masjid-i-Suleiman, Persia.

reported it was a 'terribly slow business'. He drove his men hard and had no sympathy for idleness – 'He should have brought his mother out,' he said scathingly of one driller – but he could do nothing to stop work being delayed by sickness from drinking 'what is best described as water with dung in suspension', fuel shortages and wet weather which caused the sides of the well to cave in. There was also constant trouble with the Bakhtiari, who squeezed another £500 a year out of the syndicate in return for preserving 'friendly relations'.

The real problem, however, was the failure to find oil. By the end of May 1907 Reynolds admitted: 'I can readily understand that the question "When do you expect to strike oil?" is on the lips of all those interested in the success of this undertaking, but it is one I find exceedingly difficult to answer.' Burmah Oil's chief geologist, Cunningham Craig, visited Shardin six months later when both wells were near 2,000 ft to find Reynolds certain that further drilling there was pointless. Craig agreed with him. This left one last hope, the oil shows at Maidan-i-Naftun, the 'field of naphtha'.

Reynolds had been convinced that the area near Masjid-i-Suleiman was the best prospect, ever since he had visited it nearly four years earlier. At the end of 1906 he went there again and saw 'unmistakable signs of oil'. Three weeks later he wrote to the Syndicate: 'I came out here to see this business through and unless you let me drill there I shall not think I have done so.'

The original programme for the south had been, in fact, to explore both

Construction of the road to Masjid-i-Suleiman, 1907.

prospects. Work on a link road to Masjid-i-Suleiman began in August 1906. December rains turned the Karun River into a torrent and completely demolished everything done on the road. Reynolds drafted all available staff on to the job of making good the damage and the road was completed in time to take plant up to Maidan-i-Naftun before the November rains.

At last Reynolds was instructed to 'push ahead with two selected sites [at] Masjid-i-Suleiman'. Drilling of the first well began late in January 1908 and the second in March.

Everyone was aware that the two holes were the syndicate's last chance. James Hamilton, Burmah Oil's general manager in London, told D'Arcy that the money earmarked for Persia was exhausted and he would have to put up more money himself. D'Arcy decided he did not believe him. He knew that Burmah Oil, 'for their own protection, [have] either to prove Persia a success or no good to anyone else'. His gamble paid off. By mid-May Burmah Oil had decided to spend another £40,000 if necessary, without involving D'Arcy. In any case, the prospect of an early outcome looked good. Redwood and Cunningham Craig, who visited Masjid-i-Suleiman in April, agreed with Reynolds that a depth of 1,500 ft should be enough to reach oil. Working conditions were atrocious, however, with sulphurous water corroding the wire ropes driving the drills and deadly gas threatening the lives of the drilling crews.

Early in May the first hole had reached 933 ft. Then the bit became unscrewed and took ten days to recover in temperatures of 110 degrees Fahrenheit in the shade. Soon after drilling began again a strong smell of oil was noticed and on 24 May 1908 Reynolds reported: 'The smell of gas continues and it can be seen rising from the hole in the sunlight.'

Two days later, at four in the morning, the drill reached 1,180 ft and a fountain of oil 25 metres high burst into the dawn sky.

17

An early wellhead from Masjid-i-Suleiman, Persia. Installed in 1911, it was sealed off in 1926. The wellhead is preserved at Britannic House, the company's London headquarters.

No. 1 discovery well at Masjid-i-Suleiman, 1908.

Chapter Two

The Field of Naphtha

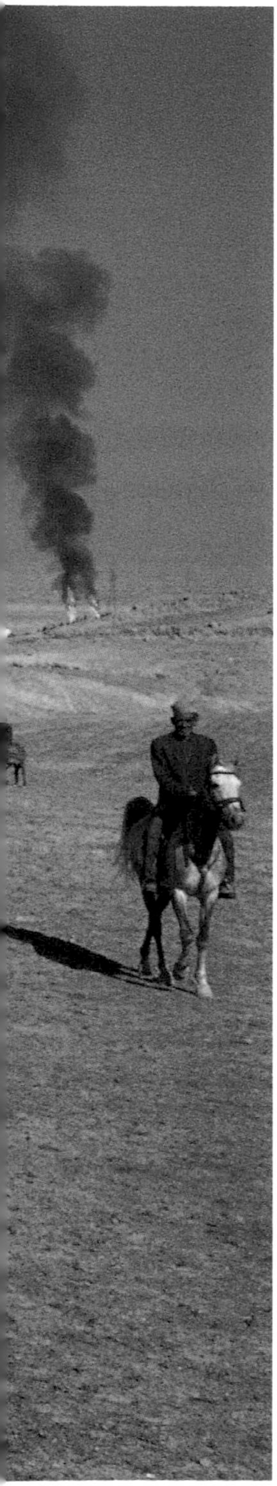

Left Qashqai horsemen on their annual migration route through central and south-west Persia. Reynolds spent much of his time haggling with nomadic tribal chiefs. Behind the horsemen natural-gas flares can be seen.

D'Arcy heard the news on 31 May. 'If this is true, all our troubles are over,' he said thankfully, but added cautiously: 'I am telling no one about it until I get the news confirmed.' Confirmation, however, was quick to arrive, with Reynolds reporting gas and then oil from the second well at Masjid-i-Suleiman. His cable ended with the words: 'There is reason to fear that pressure is entirely beyond our control.' By the end of September the last doubts were dispelled when Reynolds' assistant Bradshaw cabled to Burmah Oil's Glasgow office: 'I have to report a big strike of oil at No. 3 well at a depth of 280 ft. At 11 a.m. the 18th current, oil shot out of the well without any warning, accompanied by much gas and under great pressure.'

Boverton Redwood rushed a team of experts out to Persia and five months later reported: 'Amply sufficient work has been done to demon-

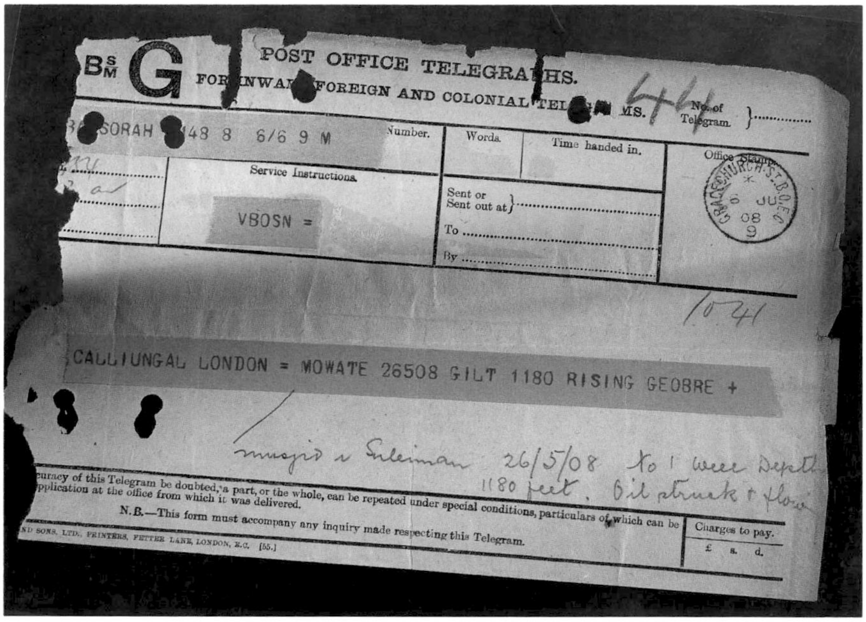

B S M G POST OFFICE TELEGRA HS.
FOR NWA FOREIGN AND COLONIAL TEL MS. 44
No. of Telegram.

SORAH 48 8 6/6 9 M

Number. Words. Time handed in. Office Stamp.

Service Instructions.

VBOSN =

Sent or Sent out at
To
By

GRACECHURCH ST. B.O.E.C. 6 JU 08 9

1041

CALLIUNGAL LONDON = MOWATE 26508 GILT 1180 RISING GEOBRE +

Musjid i Suleiman 26/5/08 No 1 Well Depth 1180 feet. Oil struck & flow

uracy of this Telegram be doubted, a part, or the whole, can be repeated under special conditions, particulars of which can be pplication at the office from which it was delivered.

N.B.—This form must accompany any inquiry made respecting this Telegram.

ND SONS, LTD., PRINTERS, FETTER LANE, LONDON, E.C. [55.]

Charges to pay. £ s. d.

Right Reynolds' cable, written in code, announces the oil strike at Masjid-i-Suleiman, 1908.

strate the existence of petroleum of good quality in abundance, at a very moderate depth, at the northern end and centre of an oil-belt extending from the Turco-Persian frontier to the Persian Gulf, and there is no doubt that many other equally promising areas of oil-bearing lands exist on the great tract of territory embraced in this unique concession.' This glowing description immediately found its way into the prospectus rapidly being written for a new company to raise capital for the development of the oilfield.

This was already at an advanced stage, with the board of the new company to include William D'Arcy and a strong Burmah element in the persons of John Cargill, Charles Wallace and James Hamilton. Lord Strathcona was chairman. Also appointed was Charles Greenway, who had just been made a director of Burmah Oil on his return from India, where he had been in charge of the company's kerosine distribution agency.

Right Agreement between D'Arcy, the Burmah Oil Company and the Concessions Syndicate.

Below The first share-issue prospectus for the Anglo-Persian Oil Company, 19 April 1909.

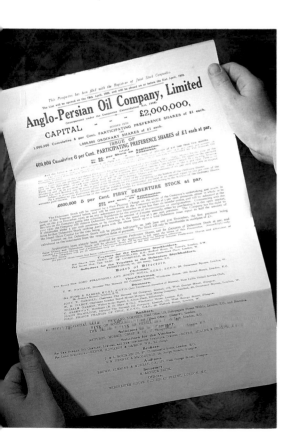

Greenway had been given the job of handling Burmah's Persian interests, beginning with writing the draft prospectus. He had also put forward the idea that D'Arcy and his associates should be rewarded not with shares in the new company but a holding in Burmah Oil itself. D'Arcy quickly agreed and settled for 170,000 Burmah Oil shares, of which 11,900 went to Vincent Kitabgi and smaller quantities to other minority shareholders including Sir Henry Drummond Wolff. As Burmah Oil's shares were priced on the London Stock Exchange at more than £5 each, the deal gave D'Arcy a clear profit of more than three-quarters of a million pounds on his Persian speculation – equal to perhaps £50m. today.

In return, Burmah Oil acquired the assets of the Concessions Syndicate and directly or indirectly ended up owning almost all the ordinary shares in the new company. D'Arcy acquired a sentimental 250 shares, which he kept until he died, Lord Strathcona bought 30,000 and 12,000 were allotted to the Bakhtiari khans under their original agreement with the syndicate.

The prospectus for a new company called the Anglo-Persian Oil Company, with a capital of one million £1 ordinary shares and one million £1 6-per-cent preference shares, was issued on 19 April 1909. Subscription lists were opened simultaneously in London and Glasgow for 600,000 of the preference shares and 600,000 5-per-cent £1 debentures. A delighted John Cargill wrote to Charles Wallace the next day: 'Nothing like

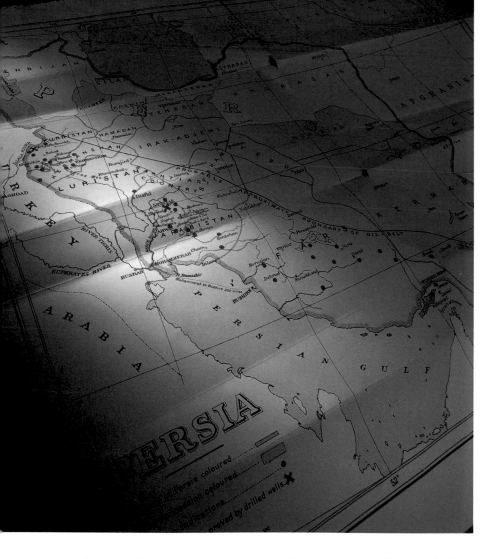

Early map of Persia, about 1908. The two red crosses indicate where oil wells were already being drilled.

the rush of applications yesterday has ever been known in Glasgow before, it being impossible at times to get inside the Bank [of Scotland] at all, and all day long the public were standing five and ten deep at the counter with their applications.'

The success of the issue, of course, owed much to the optimistic terms in which Anglo-Persian's future was described in the prospectus. Boverton Redwood, for example, had gone so far as to say: 'In the central field the operations have passed from the stage of exploration or prospecting to that of exploitation or development and the foundation of a commercial enterprise has been laid.'

The directors were equally optimistic about market prospects in East Africa, the South African colonies, Madagascar, Persia itself and countries as far away as China, Japan and Australia. If this were not enough: 'It is anticipated that an almost limitless market will be found for fuel oil for marine purposes, owing to the many advantages of oil fuel over coal, especially on Warships . . . The development of these fields is therefore calculated to be of immense benefit to the British Navy, and substantial contracts for oil fuel may be confidently looked for from the Admiralty as soon as the Company's works are in a sufficiently forward state to enable it to enter into them.'

What the prospectus did not stress was that reaching this state was a long way off. For a start, the new company needed some effective

Right A group of Bakhtiari wait to be treated by Dr Morris Young, the company's doctor.

Bakhtiari girls in modern times.

Dr Young (left) picnics with the local British Consul and his wife in Persia, 1912.

management of its own. Lacking an established organization, Anglo-Persian drew heavily on Burmah Oil for managerial experience and expertise. James Hamilton in Glasgow was put in charge of technical and accounting matters, while concessionary affairs and general co-ordination were made the responsibility of London-based Wallace, assisted by Greenway.

These arrangements did not address the need for an effective local organization in Persia. For that, Anglo-Persian followed the example of Burmah Oil, which entrusted the management of its operations in Burma to a firm of managing agents. Anglo-Persian gave the firm of Lloyd, Scott & Co. the job of handling its affairs in Persia, subject to the direction of the board in England. In return, Lloyd, Scott & Co. was granted a commission of 5 per cent on direct sales and 2.5 per cent on sales made through sub-agents. John Lloyd and Charles Walpole were released by Shaw, Wallace & Co., Burmah Oil's agents in India, to set up Lloyd, Scott & Co. in Mohammerah.

Its decision to employ a managing agency set the tone for Anglo-Persian's early years in Persia: hierarchical, deferential, paternalistic, tinged with Indian associations and the image of the Raj.

In the meantime, work proceeded on the Persian oil find. When the *Daily Telegraph* correspondent, Percy Landon, visited Masjid-i-Suleiman in autumn 1908, he found some well-built drillers' houses, rough-and-ready workshops, offices, and stables, and a primitive fort housing the platoon of Indian soldiers from the British Consulate which had replaced the unreliable Bakhtiari guards. Not so easily seen were the 'sardabs' or 'shabadans' cut into the hillsides, in which the European staff sheltered from the midday summer heat of 120 degrees Fahrenheit in the shade. Clearly visible, though, was the stone dispensary where Dr Morris Young treated the workforce for industrial injuries and an endless queue of locals for complaints in which, he wrote: 'Western medicine has little more than an antiquarian interest. Men wasted by long-continuing dysentery; women with serious breast affections; children with the characteristic disfigurement of serious chronic malaria, which would be grotesque if it were not so pitiable.' But Landon saw little except the petroleum saturating the entire area.

Masjid-i-Suleiman was almost drowning in oil and every new well increased the flood. A pipeline and a refinery were urgently needed. A Scottish engineer named Charles Ritchie, who had already worked for Burmah Oil in the East, surveyed the winding 130-mile route from the oil-fields through the mountains and along the Karun River to the island of Abadan, just below Basra. Sixty miles of six-inch pipe and 80 miles of eight-inch pipe were shipped from the USA to Abadan. Ritchie then floated the pipe sections up the Karun in barges, ignoring a local transport monopoly to the rage of its owner and of the government in Tehran. Finally teams of mules, helped by a thousand coolies, dragged them over gradients as steep as one in three. By the end of April 1911 the pipeline was completed all the way from a new pumping station at Tembi, a high point a few miles south of Masjid-i-Suleiman, to the banks of the Bahmashir River, which divided the island of Abadan from the Persian mainland.

There progress on a refinery had also been achieved. Abadan belonged to the Sheikh of Mohammerah, a small town at the north end of the island. The Sheikh was, like everyone else in Persia, short of money. By the middle of 1909 George Reynolds had persuaded him, with the help of a judicious 'gift' to his confidential adviser, to lease a site for the refinery on Abadan. The rent was £650 a year, payable in advance every ten years – in effect a down-payment of £6,500.

The winter of 1909 was spent designing a jetty and building brick-works and a bungalow, christened the Castle, for the first works manager, Norman Ramsay, who arrived from Burma with three European assistants in May 1910. Burmah Oil also sent over a team of trained workers from its Rangoon refinery. More than 250 fitters, riveters, masons and clerks followed from India, plus a score of Chinese carpenters and 30 semi-skilled

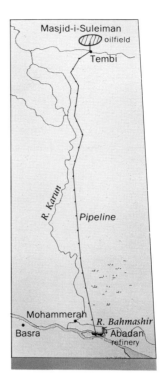

Pipeline route from Masjid-i-Suleiman to Abadan. The pipeline was completed in 1911.

Transporting pipeline sections on iron-wheeled 'jims' drawn by mules. In 1910, more than 6,000 mules were used to build the pipeline.

Crossing the Tembi River on an early route to the oilfield and (main picture) a modern photograph of similar terrain in the Zagros mountains, near Shiraz. The company spent its early years battling with the logistics of moving heavy equipment to the oilfield, across a landscape that had no roads or supply routes.

Mesopotamian Arabs. The influx of foreigners upset the Persian authorities and Charles Greenway had to warn the Mohammerah office: 'I am afraid there will be serious difficulties unless you can satisfactorily justify the employment of so many aliens.'

Greenway and James Hamilton visited Abadan early in 1911 and found progress 'in every way satisfactory. The jetty . . . was very nearly ready for use and good progress was being made with erection of buildings, machinery, tanks, etc.'

The refinery, the report added, was expected to be up and running by the end of the year. It was an over-optimistic estimate. A strike in the UK delayed delivery of essential machinery and there were shortages of materials and skilled labour in Abadan. An outbreak of cholera in the summer did not help, panicking many of the Indian workers. It was September 1912 before the first trial run could be made and that was a near-disaster. Poor bonding caused the firebrick linings and arches of the furnaces to collapse, suction trouble stopped the pumps working, and there were serious leaks in some joints. Several more months passed before the refinery was in production.

In the spring of 1910, however, these difficulties were unforeseen. What was causing concern was lack of progress at Masjid-i-Suleiman. Reports of disorganization and unhappiness had been reaching the UK for several months, since Reynolds had returned to Persia as manager of the oilfields the previous year. He was deeply angered to find himself subordinate to the new managing agency at Mohammerah and refused to co-operate with it. He stopped reporting on progress at Masjid-i-Suleiman and abandoned the job of 'political agent' to the Bakhtiari khans.

Greenway quickly became worried. As early as March 1910 he was writing: 'I am very disappointed with R and were he anyone else I should have wired our instructions for his instant dismissal . . . His attitude shows a very regrettable disregard of the Co's interest and this, combined with his advancing years, make it very desirable that we should look about for a successor.'

Reynolds' past achievements earned him a stay of execution. But at the beginning of November 1910 Greenway demanded an assurance that all necessary work on the field would be completed before the pipeline and refinery were finished. Reynolds' reply arrived a month later. It was judged inadequate and the board instructed him to return to England at once to account for himself. Three days out from Mohammerah, he passed Greenway and Hamilton travelling in the opposite direction.

Greenway reported to the board on 28 April 1911: 'We were extremely disappointed to find that Mr Reynolds had since his return to Persia in November 1909 made little or no progress with drilling and field development work or with the building of staff quarters, coolie lines, club and other necessary work', adding that 'this neglect was an attempt on the part of Mr Reynolds to delay the Company's operations with a view to placing the Company in difficulties, whereby he hoped eventually to secure the post of General Manager.' He added: 'It is with much regret that we have to write in these terms of Mr Reynolds' shortcomings, because our visit to Persia made us realize more than ever the magnificent work that he did in the pioneering stages.'

It was a valediction. Reynolds had long since been interviewed by Charles Wallace in London and, following an exchange of letters, his agreement was broken 'by mutual consent' on 15 February 1911. He received his salary up to date and a bonus of £1,000. His place was taken by Charles Ritchie.

By May 1911, 11 wells had been drilled down to the oil reservoir. Early in October Ritchie reported that production from the four wells open was 30,000 barrels a month and that he could supply Abadan with 60,000 barrels if he were given a fortnight's notice. A few days later the first 15,000 barrels of crude oil from Masjid-i-Suleiman were pumped through the pipeline to Abadan.

Eighteen months later the company's resident agent in Mohammerah, Charles Walpole, drove up to Masjid-i-Suleiman in his car in a mere nine hours. 'The staff quarters, club etc. are as comfortable as anything at Abadan,' he reported. 'The stores are well arranged and looked after and the workshop, machinery etc. run smoothly and are well kept up . . . Ritchie certainly gets things done.'

By then the initial problems at the refinery had been dealt with, but not a more fundamental one. As Percy Landon had reported so graphically on his visit, the new Persian oil smelled 'like a cataract of bad eggs' owing to its high sulphur content. None of the conventional refining processes of the time was fully removing the vile odour. This was a considerable barrier to the widespread domestic sales of kerosine so confidently forecast in the prospectus, even though Walpole reported that 'the little oil we have been able to put on the local markets has been immensely popular.'

The only solution was to sell to another company some of the huge quantities of crude that were already threatening to burst out of the oilfield. In April 1912 Greenway agreed to supply Royal Dutch-Shell's eastern distribution subsidiary, Asiatic Petroleum, with 350,000 barrels a year for the next ten years at a price of two shillings (10p) a barrel, free on board at Abadan. A further contract for refined motor spirit and kerosine was signed a few months later.

The deal all but stuck in his board's collective throat. Royal Dutch-Shell was Burmah Oil's most feared competitor in the Far East. It had already made several tentative efforts to acquire an interest in Persia, and was also making a serious attempt to muscle in on the concession in neighbouring Mesopotamia that Anglo-Persian was struggling to secure for itself.

But once again the money was running out and any customer was better than none. The first cargo of Persian crude to be shipped from Abadan, a total of 15,000 barrels, left on 23 May 1912 in the *Sultan van Koetei*, under charter to Royal Dutch-Shell.

Charles, later Lord, Greenway at Sar-i-Pul, on his way from Chiah Surkh to Tehran, 1911. He became a director of Anglo-Persian in 1909 and chairman in 1914.

Pay-day at Masjid-i-Suleiman, 1910.

The SS *Anatolia*, the first ship to dock at the Abadan jetty, 1911.

Right Winston Churchill was appointed First Lord of the Admiralty in 1911. An enthusiastic convert to oil as the most effective fuel for naval ships, he became a powerful ally of the Anglo-Persian Oil Company

Chapter Three

Fuel and the Navy

Above The supremacy of the Navy was central to Britain's war strategy. This painting, by Sir John Lewes, depicts the destruction of the German raider *Leopard* by HMS *Achilles* and HMS *Dundee* in 1918.

The sight of their first shipment sailing into the sunset may have given the workers at Abadan a sense of achievement, but the payment that eventually arrived in the company's third-floor London offices in Winchester House, Old Broad Street – rather less than £1,700 – did little to encourage the directors of Anglo-Persian. The truth was that the company was all but bankrupt. The money raised three years earlier had all gone, as had another £300,000 raised through the issue of more preference shares (many of them taken up by William Knox D'Arcy). Burmah Oil's chairman, John Cargill, was particularly despondent. 'This Persian business seems to get more complicated every day,' he complained.

Only one hope remained – the 'substantial contracts' for fuel oil for the Admiralty forecast in the prospectus. What had happened to these?

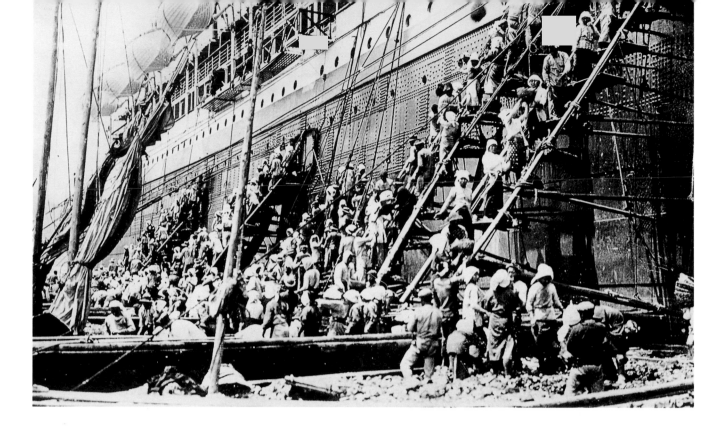

Coaling ship, 1910. Coal-burning ships usually had to dock to refuel, which was a laborious and dirty job. In contrast, oil-fuelled ships were easier and cleaner to refuel, whether in dock or at sea. They were faster and had greater range, and oil required less storage space on board.

Oil-powered World War I battleships, *Royal Sovereign*, *Revenge* and *Resolution*.

They were tantalizingly close. The Admiralty had already built or was building 56 destroyers and 74 submarines driven by oil, but it was still not convinced that it should base Britain's naval supremacy on oil. In October 1911 Winston Churchill was appointed First Lord of the Admiralty and suddenly everything was changing. Churchill had been converted by Admiral Fisher into a passionate believer in fuel oil for the Navy. Within weeks of his appointment as Anglo-Persian's chairman, Lord Strathcona had been called in to tell an Admiralty committee that the Persian oilfields were 'practically inexhaustible'.

In June 1912 a Royal Commission on oil supply was set up, with Fisher as its chairman, and by September Greenway was actively negotiating with Admiralty officials. 'The Admiralty are evidently very anxious to preserve Persia for all time as a source of supply of fuel oil for the British Navy,' he reported to Cargill.

Late in November he went to a meeting of the Royal Commission. 'All the members were most sympathetic and Lord Fisher after it was over kept me talking in Pall Mall for a considerable time. He is most emphatic that something must be done at once – both to secure Mesopotamia and to maintain British control over Anglo-Persian,' he told D'Arcy. 'From what was said, it looks as if the government have practically made up their minds to agree to our proposals.' He was being optimistic. The Admiralty did sign a contract to buy 200,000 barrels of fuel oil, but there was less support for his real target – the injection of a large sum of government money into Anglo-Persian's empty coffers.

Greenway raised the stakes by revealing that Royal Dutch-Shell had offered to buy a controlling stake in his company, playing unscrupulously on the remote risk of foreign control that this implied. The tactic worked. By July 1913 the only question remaining was how the government would provide the company with financial assistance.

The Admiralty decided to send out an expert commission to assess the risks. The key members were Rear-Admiral Sir Edmond Slade, a former Director of Naval Intelligence, and John Cadman, Professor of Mining at Birmingham University and petroleum adviser to the Colonial Office. They arrived at Mohammerah on 23 October and within three weeks Walpole cabled: 'Admiral has informed me confidentially that the Commission quite satisfied with oilfields production also Refinery.'

The commission submitted its final report in April 1914. It was a formality. Six weeks later, on 20 May, the company signed two agreements with the British government. Under the first, the government injected £2m. of new capital into Anglo-Persian, in return for a majority shareholding and the right to appoint two directors to the board. A letter from Sir John Bradbury, Joint Permanent Secretary of the Treasury, stated that, despite its large shareholding, the government would not interfere in Anglo-Persian's normal commercial operations. But it could not be denied that the government's shareholding introduced a greatly heightened political dimension to Anglo-Persian's affairs.

The second agreement was a contract for 40 million barrels of fuel oil to be delivered to the Admiralty over the next 20 years, starting on 1 July 1914 at 350,000 barrels a year and rising to a maximum of 3.5 million barrels a year. Parliamentary approval, however, was not guaranteed. An article in *The Times* warned that 'the oil wells of the Royal Navy will be an abiding temptation in times of trouble,' and concluded that parliament 'should not vote the money and sanction this possibly perilous experiment without the fullest and frankest explanation, not only of the views of Mr Churchill but still more of those of the Foreign Office.'

On 17 June Winston Churchill obliged. He asked the House of Commons to pass the 'Anglo-Persian Oil Company, Acquisition of Capital Bill' because 'The oil consumer has not got freedom of choice in regard to other alternative fuels, but neither has he freedom of choice in regard to the sources of supply from which he can purchase. Look out upon the wide expanse of the oil regions of the world! Two gigantic corporations – one in either hemisphere – stand out predominantly. In the New World there is the Standard Oil, against which the Cowdray interests maintain by war and by negotiation a very powerful but semi-independent life. In the Old World the great combination of Shell and the Royal Dutch, with all their subsidiary and ancillary branches, has practically covered the whole ground and has even reached out into the New World. Against this, amongst British companies who have maintained an independent existence, the Burmah Oil Company, with its offshoot the Anglo-Persian Oil Company, is almost the only noticeable feature.' Churchill was backed up by Sir Edward Grey, the Foreign Secretary, and the resolution passed by 191 votes to 67.

For Greenway, the government's injection of new capital and the Admiralty contract represented a major coup. He had acquired desperately needed finance, while simultaneously diluting Burmah Oil's shareholding and avoiding the predatory grasp of Royal Dutch-Shell – and all without

29

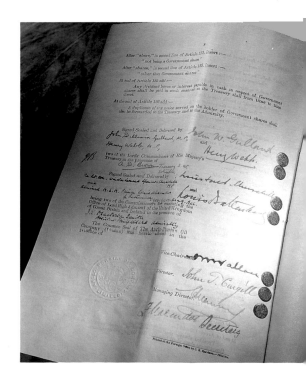

Anglo Persian signed a contract with the British government to supply the Admiralty with oil for a period of 20 years, starting in 1914. Winston Churchill put his signature to the document as First Lord of the Admiralty.

The oil-pumping station at Tembi, about 1916. In the foreground is an encampment of Indian Army troops who guarded the installation.

The British sloop HMS *Odin* (shown here) together with HMS *Espiègle* played a vital part in removing the threat of attack by the Turkish Army on Anglo-Persian's refinery at Abadan.

conceding managerial control. The commercial survival and independence of Anglo-Persian were assured.

The government's investment in Persian oil could not have been better timed. The Emperor Franz Josef's heir, the Archduke Franz Ferdinand, was assassinated in Sarajevo on 28 June. Six weeks later Germany launched a full-scale attack on France and the Great War had begun.

Turkey took Germany's side, commandeering the company's stocks of kerosine in Baghdad and Basra, while the crew of a German liner blockaded in Basra filled a number of small vessels with sand, ready to sink them at the mouth of the Shatt-al-Arab. HMS *Odin* was ordered to patrol the river to prevent this. She was joined by another sloop, HMS *Espiègle*, at the end of September, by which time Turkish troops had camped opposite the refinery.

Britain finally declared war on Turkey on 5 November. The next day *Espiègle* steamed provocatively past the Turks and, when they opened fire, shot up their trenches and put them to flight. At the same time *Odin* and other warships silenced a Turkish fort at the mouth of the Shatt-al-Arab. Two days later an expeditionary force landed on the Turkish side of the river, while a company of Indian troops disembarked at Abadan to protect the refinery. A Turkish counter-attack was repulsed and by 21 November the British had taken Basra. The direct threat to the refinery was over.

Defeated in the field, the Turks tried to incite a holy war against the British by Persian Arabs. They managed to provoke the Bawi tribe into cutting the oil pipeline in two places north of Ahwaz early in February and it took the company four months to repair the damage. Supplies to Abadan fell by 600,000 barrels during the period and a million barrels were burned at the oilfield for lack of storage.

The Turks and their Arab allies also threatened the oilfield itself until they were defeated north of Ahwaz in March and again near Basra in April.

Persia remained a battleground for some time, with a British force posted to Tembi to counter possible enemy action as late as November 1917. Dissident tribesmen also made various attacks on the company's employees and assets, mostly for loot. But the more powerful Bakhtiari khans continued to defend its operations, due partly to the diplomacy of Dr Young and partly to direct payments to the local guards.

In the meantime Anglo-Persian's operations expanded in leaps and bounds. Crude oil supplies were not an issue. The problem was keeping the flow under control, particularly since well F7 had suddenly increased its output from 1,000 to 10,000 barrels a day, equal to a potential four million barrels a year all on its own. Big increases in pipeline and refining capacity would be needed to enable the company to honour its commitments to the Royal Navy.

Material for a new ten-inch pipeline was delivered late in 1914, but the war-torn state of the country and the heavy demands made by the Expeditionary Force on the company's transport prevented this being completely laid until January 1917.

The expansion of the Abadan refinery was similarly delayed. Most of the material for four new 'benches' of stills, extensions to the power station and treatment plant, and new storage tanks and jetties, arrived at Abadan early in 1915. But again the military's requirements came first. The refinery staff were initially ordered to construct gunshields and armour-plating for naval warships and then to assemble 16 'Fly' and four 'Moth' gunboats shipped in pieces from the UK.

In spite of this war work and with only 50 European staff to manage 1,200 unhappy expatriate Indians and more than a thousand undisciplined and unskilled tribal workers, the refinery's manager, R G Neilson, succeeded in raising production from 200,000 barrels in 1913 to nearly 3.5 million barrels by 1917. Further development increased output at Abadan to more than five million barrels by the end of the war the following year. Some of this, of course, was oil for the Navy. Altogether the company supplied the military, including the forces in the Middle East, with more than seven million barrels of fuel oil during the Great War.

Not all of it was of very good quality. The Navy was particularly critical of the viscosity of Abadan fuel oil, which made it hard to use in colder climates. Greenway engaged Dr Alfred Dunstan, a specialist in the viscosity of fluids, to investigate the nature of Persian crude and the problems of refining it. Dunstan visited Persia in 1916 and the following year the company purchased a Georgian mansion near Sunbury-on-Thames, England, as a research centre, with Dunstan in charge.

Shipping was another challenge. Thanks to its fast, powerful new ships, the Royal Navy established an early dominance over the German Imperial Navy. The Battle of Jutland left Great Britain in total control of

Bakhtiari tribesmen with guns. The calming influence of Dr Morris Young, who took this photograph in the 1920s, helped to ensure that the Bakhtiari khans remained loyal to the company during World War I.

32 An oil storage tank holed by a shell from a German cruiser, Madras, 1914.

the seas until Admiral von Tirpitz launched his desperate submarine attacks in 1916 and 1917.

But the outbreak of war drove freight rates sky-high. By the end of 1914 Charles Greenway, who had become chairman of Anglo-Persian the previous July, decided that the company must have its own tanker fleet. Orders were placed with Armstrong Whitworth and Swan Hunter for one 5,000-ton and three 10,000-ton tankers, and a captured German vessel was bought from the Admiralty for £55,000. In April 1915 a new subsidiary, the British Tanker Company, was formed to take over the growing fleet, with Lord Inchcape and Admiral Slade as *ex officio* directors. By 1918 British Tanker's tonnage had risen to 150,000 and many of its ships were very profitably employed.

Meanwhile, Greenway had seized the opportunity presented by the war to acquire a ready-made British distribution and sales organization. The

company in question, formed in 1906, was a subsidiary of the German-owned Europäische Petroleum Union. It had acquired an exclusive agency to sell Shell motor spirit in the UK, and by 1914 employed nearly 3,000 people and had 36 per cent of the British petrol market. Only the Anglo-American Oil Company, the British subsidiary of Standard Oil (New Jersey), had a larger market share. Because of its German parentage, the company was classified as an enemy concern and placed in the hands of the Public Trustee for Enemy Property, from whom Greenway bought it in 1917.

The company's name was British Petroleum.

The *British Maple*, bought in 1919 by Anglo-Persian's new shipping subsidiary, the British Tanker Company.

Early lamp-oil delivery wagon of the British Petroleum Company, bought by Anglo-Persian in 1917.

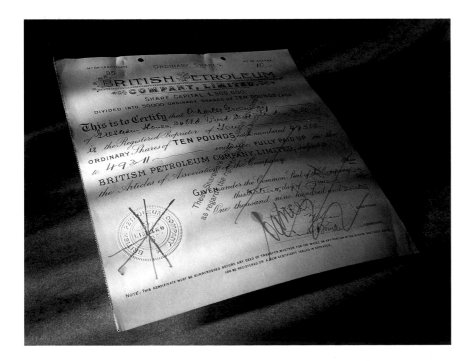

Left British Petroleum Company share certificate, issued to Charles Greenway in 1917 and later cancelled.

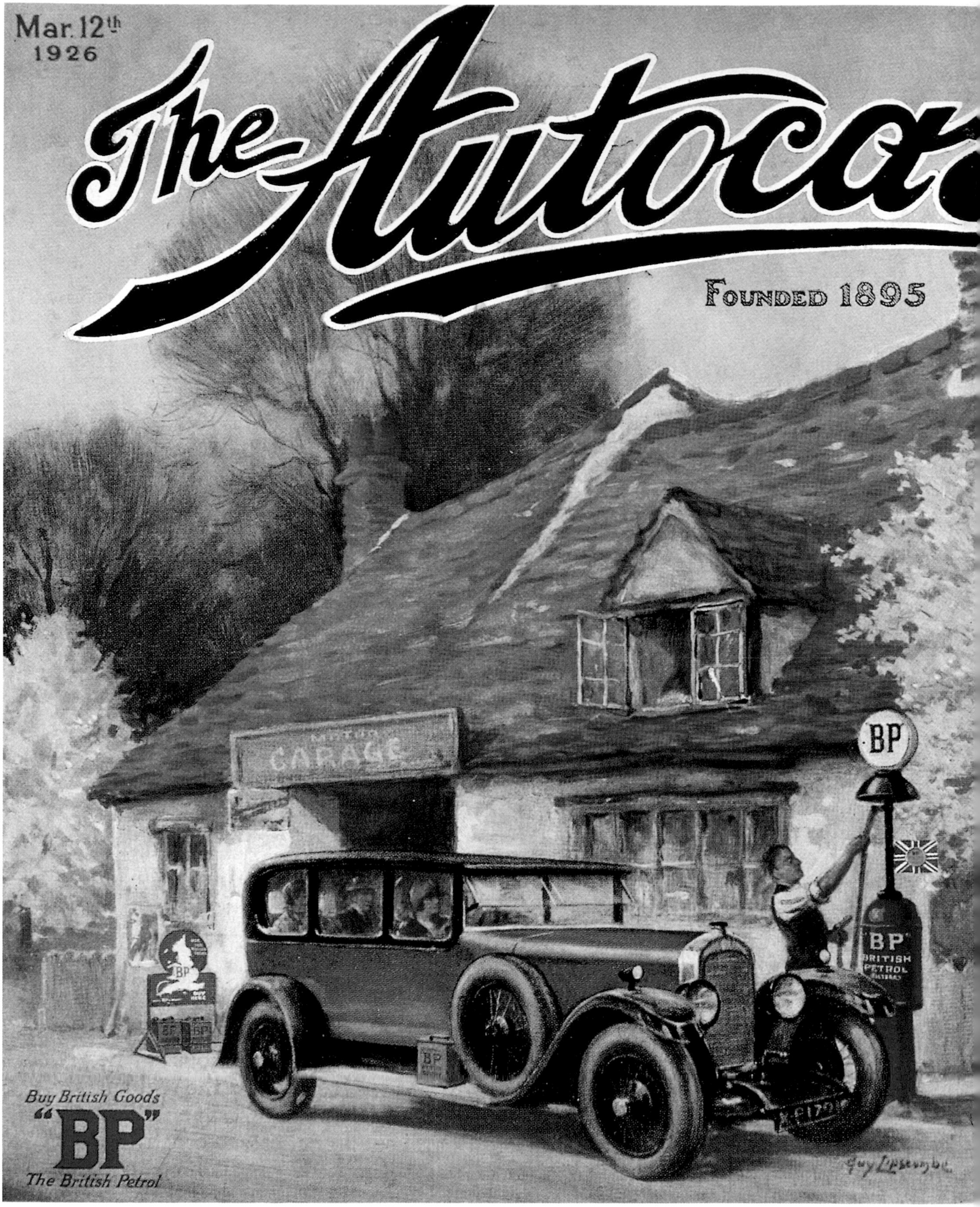
Mar. 12th
1926
The Autocar
Founded 1895
GARAGE
BP
"BP"
BRITISH
PETROL
Buy British Goods
"BP"
The British Petrol
Guy Lipscombe

Chapter Four

An Absolutely Self-Contained Organization

Anglo-Persian emerged from the war a vastly bigger and richer company than four years earlier. In mid-1914 the company was producing only 5,600 barrels a day of crude oil and operating an inefficient and unreliable refinery that yielded products of inferior quality. It owned no marketing facilities or tanker fleet and relied on contracts with Royal Dutch-Shell and the British Admiralty for its sales. It was operating at a loss and had paid no dividends to its shareholders.

By the end of 1918, in contrast, daily crude oil production had risen to more than 18,000 barrels. The Abadan refinery was turning out 16,000 barrels a day of refined products and Anglo-Persian had formed its own tanker company, created a research centre and acquired a marketing organization. Most of this expansion had been financed internally as Anglo-Persian moved into the black, making its first trading profit in 1915 and paying its first dividend to ordinary shareholders in 1917.

These wartime developments brought the company closer to the achievement of Greenway's vision of creating 'an absolutely self-contained organization' – a vertically integrated corporation, engaged in every sector of the oil industry from the wellhead to the consumer, encompassing crude production, transportation, refining and retail marketing.

Before World War I, almost all Anglo-Persian's fixed assets were in Persia – in the oilfield, in the pipeline and at Abadan. By 1918, after the heavy wartime investment in tankers and marketing facilities, about half the company's fixed assets were outside Persia, mainly in the downstream sector of the business. Even so, it was still some way from being regarded as one of the world's leading international oil groups. This required investment far beyond Anglo-Persian's income from its existing operations. The company turned to the capital market for much of the finance needed for expansion in the five years after the war. Most of the investment was in tankers, refineries and marketing outlets, mainly outside Persia. By the mid-1920s little more than a third of Anglo-Persian's fixed assets were in Persia, but the country remained by far its largest centre of operations.

At the end of the war, the company still had much to learn about its vast oil discovery at Masjid-i-Suleiman. By 1919 there were 48 wells producing around 19,000 barrels a day. This was not nearly enough, in the opinion of Duncan Garrow, the company's new technical director, to meet demand, which he put at 38,000 barrels a day in the short term, rising to 77,000 barrels a few years later. Garrow recommended a five-year crash drilling programme of 123 wells. R R Thompson, the oilfield's manager throughout the war, strongly disagreed. He had observed that gas pressure was constant throughout the field and had concluded that this proved it

The 1920s saw the start of international BP branding and advertising. It was a period of economic expansion when the numbers of light aircraft, motor cars and commercial vehicles increased rapidly.

36 Model of the tanker, the *British Merchant*, which was built in 1922. The company invested heavily in the downstream sector of the business after World War I.

Early BP road tanker.

was a continuous structure. 'If the central wells do draw their production from the whole of the oil-producing rocks of the field,' he argued, 'it would obviously be a waste of money and very possibly a waste of gas energy to drill any more wells into the oil reservoir.'

It was a revolutionary approach. But Thompson reminded the board that in 'no other proved oil-bearing territory has the development been under the control of one management'. Everywhere else in the world 'the sole idea of the various interested companies has been an anxiety to tap the oil horizon before their rivals, regardless of the damage done to the oil-bearing strata by faulty drilling to the detriment of the prolonged productive capacity of the field.'

John Cadman, appointed the company's technical adviser in 1921, thought Thompson was probably right, but it took another two years before he could report with certainty that the Masjid-i-Suleiman field was a 'single dynamic unit'. The only question was how long its apparently limitless reserves would last. It was a worry that, in spite of widespread exploration, Anglo-Persian was still dependent on the one oilfield at Masjid-i-Suleiman for all its crude production. Cadman asked an eminent Hungarian geologist, Professor Hugo de Böckh, to choose new exploration sites. De Böckh made two visits to Persia in 1923 and 1924 and then recommended drilling in six places. Oil was found in commercial quantities at four of them and three, Haft Kel, Agha Jari and Gach Saran, proved to be giant structures comparable to Masjid-i-Suleiman. Any fears that the company would run out of oil were extinguished.

Abadan was another problem area. The drive to maximize production during the war had left the refinery in poor condition. Garrow had suggested that output should be frozen at around 19,000 barrels a day 'until we have every department, including shipping and marketing, in thorough

The usual method of transport in Persia and Iraq. A mule carries cases of oil under the 'Palm Tree' brand.

Naft-i-Iran (meaning 'Oil of Iran') was published in July 1924 for Anglo-Persian staff. It was the first of the company's publications and the precursor of today's *Shield* magazine.

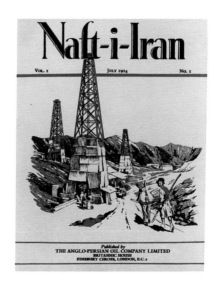

proportion all round, properly organized as there is, in my opinion, sufficient work ahead of Abadan in construction work to last them at least two years'. His advice was not taken and Abadan's production had doubled by 1922. But bad management and a disastrous fire caused a collapse in output to 13,500 barrels a day in 1923, leaving the refinery 'a crippled plant'. Labour relations were also in a poor state. Strikes by the Indian, Arab and Persian workers in December 1920 were ended only by 80-per-cent wage rises and improvements in living and working conditions.

The Indian workers remained unhappy and many were sent home after another strike 15 months later. This left Abadan short of skilled workers and efforts began to be made to train Persians. These included building training workshops at Abadan and providing scholarships to university courses in the UK for the most promising. However, there was a sharp contrast between the living standards of native employees and the white expatriate staff.

The growing European community had its complaints, but there was little real discontent once housing improved and better medical facilities were provided. Concerts, amateur dramatics, sports, parties and of course servants alleviated the stress of living under an alien sun. The company even recruited a gardener from Kew Botanic Gardens in London.

When Cadman visited Abadan late in 1924, his criticism of the state of the refinery was sharp. 'During the last five years adjustment under post-war conditions to any settled form of policy has been lamentably slow and the Refinery . . . is far from being stabilized on a sound profit-earning basis . . . Abadan, as it exists today, is not a refinery in the proper sense of the word, but merely a gigantic topping or distillation plant.' It took new management and heavy investment in modern American plant to turn Abadan into an efficient operation.

Anglo-Persian's oil interests in the Middle East were not confined to

Persia. Its involvement in neighbouring Mesopotamia (Iraq from 1920) dated back to 1901. As soon as Alfred Marriott returned to England from Tehran, D'Arcy dispatched him to Constantinople to seek an oil concession from the Sultan. This time Marriott had failed. D'Arcy, however, persevered, as later did Greenway. After labyrinthine negotiations between rival oil companies and governments of various nationalities, a concession

38 Kashguli khans entertain members of the company's staff in Persia, 1925.

Kurdistan, Iraq. After the discovery of the immense Kirkuk field in 1927, Iraq became one of the most valuable concessionary areas in the world.

covering most of Iraq was granted in 1925 to the Turkish Petroleum Company, in which Anglo-Persian held a 47.5-per-cent interest. The other shareholders were Royal Dutch-Shell, the French-owned Compagnie Française des Pétroles, and a remarkable Armenian entrepreneur named Calouste Gulbenkian, whose share in the Turkish Petroleum Company earned him the nickname 'Mr Five Percent'.

Herbert Nichols, one of Anglo-Persian's directors, was made managing director and acting chairman of the Turkish Petroleum Company. Optimistic about the oil prospects in Iraq, he appointed a nucleus of staff, opened an office in Gresham Street, London, and sent Professor Hugo de Böckh on a geological mission to Iraq. Drilling rigs, staff and equipment were sent out and the first well was begun in the presence of King Faisal in April 1927. On 15 October a rig at Baba Gurgur, immediately north of Kirkuk, made a spectacular strike of oil, which flowed with such force that it was uncontrollable for several days. The discovery of the immense Kirkuk field transformed Iraq into one of the most valuable concessionary areas in the world.

The political carve-up of the Iraqi oil concession by the imperial powers of Britain and France did not, however, suit the USA. Under pressure, the European shareholders reluctantly allowed a consortium of

American oil companies to acquire half Anglo-Persian's shareholding in 1928, reducing it to 23.75 per cent. At the same time, each of the participants in the Turkish Petroleum Company agreed to channel all their oil interests in the area of the former Turkish Empire through the Turkish Petroleum Company. A red line was drawn around the area on a map and the pact became known as the Red Line Agreement.

Oilfields, test areas, pipelines and refineries in Persia and Iraq, 1928.

39

April 1925 edition of *APOC Magazine*, the successor to *Naft-i-Iran*.

The Baba Gurgur discovery was not the first oil find in Iraq. In 1923 Anglo-Persian had discovered oil at Naft Khaneh, on territory which had been transferred from Persia to the Turkish Empire in 1913. As the transferred land had been included in D'Arcy's Persian concession, the Iraqi government recognized the company as sole operator of the Naft Khaneh oilfield. Anglo-Persian developed the field and laid a pipeline to a refinery site on the Alwand River outside Khanaqin, where refining began in 1927. Its products were marketed in Iraq by a local subsidiary of Anglo-Persian.

By then the company had broadened its international marketing interests considerably. It first ventured into continental Europe in 1919 through an interest in L'Alliance of Belgium. Over the next few years other marketing outlets were acquired or formed in Denmark, Norway, France, Italy, Switzerland, Austria, the Netherlands and Germany.

This coincided with the introduction into Europe of the American system of kerbside pumps, superseding the returnable two-gallon cans which had previously been used for sales of motor spirit. The attractions of roadside pumps were boosted by advertising, using images painted by artists such as Rex Whistler and Edward McKnight Kauffer. The winner of a staff competition for a new logo was a design placing the initials BP in black on a red shield, chosen because it symbolized solidity and protection. Soon

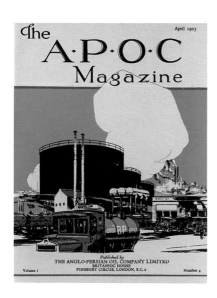

An early roadside pump in France, 1920s.

Two early examples of the BP trademark in France.

Captain Malcolm Campbell about to start his record-breaking run at Pendine Sands, Carmarthenshire, Wales, 4 February 1927. His *Bluebird*, running on BP fuel, reached a top speed of more than 180 mph.

afterwards, the company adopted green and yellow as its colours. In Britain, BP pumps, previously red, were painted green. And the new brand image was promoted by sponsoring world speed record-breaker, Malcolm Campbell.

To supply the company's European retail markets, new refineries, much smaller than that at Abadan, were brought on stream at Llandarcy in South Wales in 1921 and at Grangemouth in Scotland in 1924. Anglo-Persian's French associate also built a refinery at Courchelettes, near Douai.

On the other side of the world, Anglo-Persian and the Australian government formed Commonwealth Oil Refineries Limited, which built a new refinery at Laverton, near Melbourne, to supply oil products to the local market. The company's international marine bunkering business also opened new outlets, and Anglo-Persian went into the aviation fuel market, starting the BP Aviation Service in 1926.

By the time Greenway retired as chairman in March 1927 Anglo-Persian was producing, refining and selling nearly 100,000 barrels of oil a

Britannic House in London's
Finsbury Circus, designed by
Sir Edwin Lutyens in the early
1920s as Anglo-Persian's
headquarters, combined
practicality with architectural
beauty.

Below The development of **41**
the BP logo.

| 1919–1921 | "B.P." MOTOR SPIRIT |

day. In Persia, the managing agency system was replaced in 1922 with a
line management. By 1927 this employed 26,000 staff and labour. In
London, the staff had moved to a new head office in Finsbury Circus,
designed by Sir Edwin Lutyens. Although Anglo-Persian still held a much
smaller share of the world oil market than its principal rivals, Royal Dutch-
Shell and Standard Oil (New Jersey), it had become a major player in the
international scene.

Anglo-Persian was not the only oil company expanding its operations.
Discoveries in Mexico and Venezuela had opened up huge new fields.
Lenin's New Economic Policy had resulted in a large recovery in Russian
oil exports to European markets, including Britain. After widespread fears
of oil shortages in the early 1920s, the world was suddenly flooded with
supplies.

When Henri Deterding of Royal Dutch launched a price war against
'communist' oil, Anglo-Persian was not at first concerned by the 'insane
extent' of the price cutting. 'We can await the result with perfect
equanimity,' Greenway told shareholders in 1924, 'since for every shilling
that we lose, our competitors must lose two or more.' Two years later he
was still assuring them that 'our success in finding further outlets for our
production encourages us to continue our policy of expansion.' That did
not mean that he and his fellow directors, including the British government's two representatives, were averse to a little mutual protection. The
company had already quietly extended its relationship with Royal Dutch-
Shell through a five-year 'trading arrangement for the sale of petrol in the
United Kingdom and Ireland'.

But John Cadman, who had taken over the chair from Greenway in
1927, was about to go much further. Early in 1928 he concluded two
marketing agreements covering great tracts of territory. The first was for the
Indian market. The previous year Burmah Oil and Royal Dutch-Shell had
decided to amalgamate their marketing organizations in India into a joint

company, the Burmah-Shell Oil Storage and Distributing Company of India. Burmah Oil secured the first right to supply the new company's requirements from its crude production in India and Burma. Rights to supply the remainder were split equally between Royal Dutch-Shell and Anglo-Persian. In return, Anglo-Persian agreed not to enter the Indian market on its own account. The second agreement gave Anglo-Persian and Royal Dutch-Shell equal shares in a new joint operation, named the Consolidated Petroleum Company, to market Shell and Anglo-Persian products in a vast area

Distribution wagons of Commonwealth Oil Refineries Limited, formed in 1920 by Anglo-Persian and the Australian government.

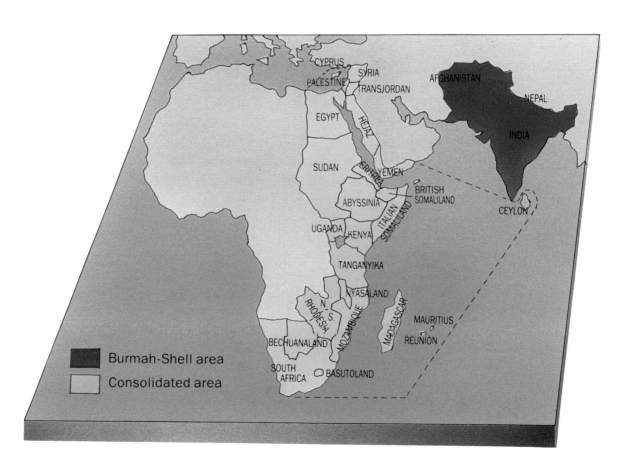

Burmah-Shell area

Consolidated area

The *Glasgow Evening News* took a somewhat cynical view of the Achnacarry meeting.

Cartoon of Lord Greenway, chairman from 1914 to 1927, immortalized in Upton Sinclair's novel, *Oil!* as 'Old Spats and Monocle'.

covering eastern and southern Africa, parts of the Middle East, and Ceylon.

A still more ambitious scheme was to come. In August 1928, Cadman was Deterding's guest at Achnacarry Castle in the Scottish highlands, along with Walter Teagle of Standard Oil (New Jersey), William Mellon of Gulf Oil and Colonel Robert Stewart of Standard Oil of Indiana. Ostensibly they were there to shoot grouse and catch salmon, but the real quarry was a formula to control world oil output by fixing the market shares of the major producers at their then current levels. The official title of the 17-page document that emerged was the 'Pool Association', but it became known almost immediately as the Achnacarry or 'As-Is' Agreement.

The agreement was only partially effective because there were too many independent sources of oil, but it confirmed the arrival of Anglo-Persian as one of the world's oil majors. The 74-year-old Baron Greenway of Stanbridge Earls, made president of Anglo-Persian after his retirement as chairman, could be forgiven for proclaiming at the annual general meeting in 1930, 'a record of development which, I am confident, has not been equalled by any other concern in the history of the world'.

Typical delivery lorry of the 1920s.

Aviation fuelling at Gloucester, England, 1928.

Chapter Five

Riza Shah Pahlavi

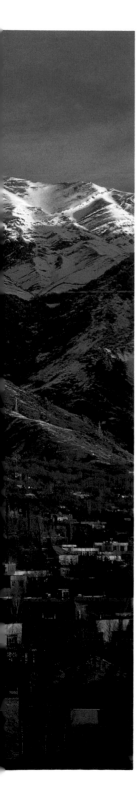

Tehran at sunrise. During the 1920s the company increasingly found itself caught in the middle of a power struggle between the central government in Tehran, led by Riza Shah Pahlavi, and the local tribal khans. Anglo-Persian had worked hard to establish good relations in south-west Persia, but they were now being threatened by Riza Shah's demands.

The world, however, was changing. The Wall Street Crash in October 1929 hamstrung the 'As-Is' Agreement as effectively as it undermined the world economy. Oil could not escape. The average price of US crude (still the world benchmark) stood at $1.88 a barrel in 1926. In 1931 it was down to 65 cents.

Anglo-Persian was forced to cut capital expenditure from £8.2m. in 1930 to £2.7m. in 1932. Head office staff, who numbered more than 1,000 in 1927, came down to fewer than 600 in 1934. The numbers employed by the company in Persia were halved from 31,000 to under 16,000.

The effect of the Depression was felt throughout Anglo-Persian's business. In Britain the market dominance of British Petroleum and the local subsidiaries of Royal Dutch-Shell and Standard Oil (New Jersey) was threatened from the mid-1920s by Russian Oil Products, which imported Russian oil and indulged in aggressive price-cutting. By 1931 competitive pressures were mounting, with Russian Oil Products, the Texas Company and Cleveland Petroleum Products all trying to increase their market shares.

To combat this competition, Anglo-Persian and Royal Dutch-Shell agreed to combine their UK marketing organizations. Shell-Mex and BP Limited came into being in 1932 with a market share of 42 per cent. Ownership of the joint operation was divided between the parent companies in proportion to their market shares. Anglo-Persian received a 40-per-cent shareholding compared with 60 per cent for Royal Dutch-Shell.

But with prices and sales volumes falling, nothing could stop Anglo-Persian's profits from collapsing from £6.5m. in 1930 to £3.1m. in 1933. Dividends were sharply reduced and so were payments to the Persian government. In June 1932 the company sent a cable to Tehran informing the Persian government that its royalty for 1931 worked out at only £300,000, a fall of £1m. from the year before.

Five months later His Imperial Majesty Riza Shah Pahlavi threw the company file in the fire and cancelled the D'Arcy Concession.

Riza Shah was a big, powerful, self-educated soldier with a domineering personality and a dangerous temper who had seized power by a military coup in 1921. On the surface, he was friendly towards Anglo-Persian. He made more than one visit to its operations and courteously 'received' its directors in his palace in Tehran. The good standing of the company was also reflected in the accommodating attitude of his ministers, who lived in justifiable terror of their autocratic master – self-exile or suicide being the only escape routes for anyone who incurred his displeasure.

Sir John Cadman, chairman of Anglo-Persian from 1927 to 1941, leaves Tehran at the conclusion of the concession negotiations, 30 April 1933.

Riza Shah (on right) visits Abadan refinery, Persia, 1930.

There were hints in the comments John Cadman began making about its role in Persia that the company realized its vulnerability. In his first year as chairman, he told shareholders: 'We want Persians to feel that our activities in Persia are not only directed towards extracting oil but also towards developing a great national industry in the country.' He admitted that the company's methods and efforts were being criticized, although he claimed that there had been no serious differences or misunderstandings with the Persian government in the past. He was being economical with the truth.

It was only six years since Anglo-Persian had paid the government £1m. in settlement of underpayments for past royalties – a fact uncovered for the Persian authorities by the British accountant, William McLintock, who found that the Persian payment was being calculated after depreciation, loan interest and British excess profits tax. McLintock had also undermined the company's attempt to persuade Persia to exchange its 16-per-cent share of net profits for a royalty of two shillings (10p) per ton by estimating that the change would have cut the state's oil revenues in 1919 from £428,000 to £138,000.

There was no suggestion that Anglo-Persian had been intentionally underpaying Persia. However, the argument contributed to a legacy of distrust which dated back to early objections by Tehran to the company's private dealings with tribal chiefs. A revised royalty agreement had been reached at the end of 1920 and had been in use ever since. But it had never been ratified, in spite of endless discussions and protestations of goodwill.

Thomas Jacks, the company's resident director in Tehran, had been one of the first to appreciate the depth of the problem. As early as 1928 he was warning the board that 'the Persian Government feels itself sufficiently well established to be able to dictate its wishes to the Company and if the Company does not react in the desired manner the intention is to hamper its operations with a view to ultimately forcing acceptance upon it by means of prevarication and passive resistance.'

It was as good an analysis as any. Although a revised draft for a new concession was agreed by the Shah's Council of Ministers at the beginning of 1932, hopes of a final settlement had been dashed by the news of the reduced royalty. Within a few weeks the Persian negotiator, the Shah's Minister of Court, Abdul Timurtash, suggested a complete revision of the concession. At the same time, Tehran newspapers began a virulent campaign against Anglo-Persian. Although the Persian government denied any responsibility for the articles, events showed that the count-down to the Shah's cancellation of the concession had begun.

The company had been expecting trouble, but not on this scale. John Cadman told the Persian Minister in London that the denunciation of the concession was 'utterly at variance with what we had been led to expect' It was, he said, 'as though we were about to sit down to a game of chess and the first player swept all the pieces off the board, then asked us to make the next move and was astonished to learn that we did not consider that was the way chess, or any other game, could possibly be played.' That said, he proceeded to play a very cool game of diplomacy.

The company had already brought the British government into play. The Under-Secretary of State for Foreign Affairs, Anthony Eden, sent a note to Tehran demanding an immediate retraction and the Cabinet authorized an appeal to the League of Nations in Geneva. This began in January 1933, but was adjourned until 'at least May' to allow for direct negotiations between the Persian government and the company. Private discussions began in Paris, but became bogged down.

Although not all his colleagues on the board agreed, Cadman decided the only hope was direct negotiations in Persia. He drafted a new concession based on the principle of a fixed royalty per ton of oil instead of a percentage of profits, and arrived in Tehran at the beginning of April with his deputy, William Fraser, and Morris Young, who was widely respected in Persia. They found a 'dreadful atmosphere', with the newspapers still full of anti-British propaganda and the local population forbidden to associate with Europeans. Cadman recorded in his diary that even ministers 'seem afraid for their necks and are almost terrified to speak or even be seen with me or any of my party'.

A meeting with the Shah on 11 April gave grounds for hope. Persia's ruler greeted Cadman cordially and claimed he 'only wanted to clean the slate'. Two days later the Persians produced a revised draft for a new concession. But by 23 April the two sides had reached deadlock yet again.

Cadman asked for another audience with the Shah the next day, at which he told him that negotiations had utterly broken down and he had come to say farewell. It may have been purely a coincidence that the company's aeroplane could be seen preparing for departure from the windows of the room in which the meeting took place. Cadman's real gamble was that Persia did not want the argument referred back to the League of Nations. The Shah replied amiably that he would not hear of his guests leaving so soon. The same afternoon he presided over a meeting which included the Prime Minister, the Minister of Finance and the Minister of Justice, at which the chief points of difference were discussed.

Two days later Riza Shah convened another meeting. Some final argument about the term of the new concession was solved by the company's agreeing to reduce its area to 100,000 sq. miles, provided it could choose which these were. And then suddenly it was all over. On 30 April John Cadman telegraphed London: 'I have agreed finally after intervention Shah as follows begins: Principal features new concession. Term 60 years from 1st January year 1933. Area 100,000 square miles to be selected before end of 1938 . . . Payment 4 shillings per ton also 20 per cent of ordinary dividends distributed to shareholders after first 5 per cent with annual guaranteed minimum £750,000 . . . All general working clauses including arbitration and surrender clauses on 2 years notice entirely satisfactory.'

Anglo-Persian's offices in Tehran, Persia, 1932.

APOC Magazine commemorates the coronation of Riza Shah Pahlavi, July 1926.

Chapter Six

Just and Fair

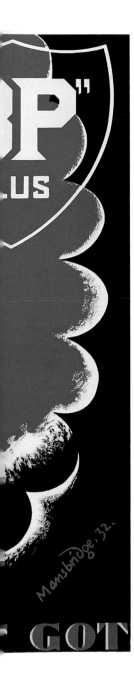

In public, Anglo-Persian presented the new concession as, if not a success, at least 'just and fair'. 'It has, it is hoped, dispelled for the future the causes of difference between the Persian Government and the Company which existed in the past,' a circular to shareholders at the end of May claimed. But John Cadman more accurately reflected British public opinion when he confided to his diary at the end of the negotiations: 'I felt we had been pretty well plucked.'

However, there were genuine grounds for an optimistic view. The terms of the new concession were much clearer, in particular the basis of payments, and the expiry date had been extended by 32 years. Not to mention the real reason for rejoicing – the fact that the company still had a Persian oil concession at all.

The reduction in its size to 100,000 sq. miles was not actually very significant. This was still larger than the whole of the United Kingdom and, as the company could choose the area it kept, meant that Anglo-Persian would include all the discoveries it had made so far in Persia, as well as its best prospects. Admittedly, the price was high. But, in truth, the company had known for some years that it would sooner or later have to pay a larger share of its oil revenue to its host.

One of the catalysts was the oil agreement reached a year earlier in Persia's western neighbour, Iraq, which had just become a member of the League of Nations. This had infuriated the Shah, who did not consider the territory with its British-created monarchy and its polyglot population deserved to be a country at all.

Cadman was scarcely more impressed. 'The Government is irresponsible from the King down and capable of anything. A Cabinet Committee has already expressed the opinion that the Concession is null and void and foolish as it may seem Government quite capable of passing a law to that effect. Cabinet Ministers continually threatening to resign and even talk of suicide,' he cabled to London on a visit to Baghdad in 1930.

Eventually a new concession was signed in 1931. One clause committed the Iraq Petroleum Company (as the Turkish Petroleum Company was renamed in 1929) to build a pipeline from the landlocked Kirkuk field to the Mediterranean Sea by the end of 1935. Political wrangling between the French and the British over whether the pipeline should terminate at Tripoli in the Lebanon or Haifa in Palestine was only ended by Iraq Petroleum's agreeing to build two pipelines. One, terminating at Tripoli, would be 532 miles long. The other, ending at Haifa, would have a length of 620 miles. Arab tribesmen watched the construction of the pipelines in the waterless Iraqi desert. The work was completed without serious mishap

The 1930s saw some exciting and colourful BP advertising. Distinguished artists such as Rex Whistler and Edward Bawden were commissioned to work on advertisements for motor spirits such as BP Plus and BP Ethyl. Catchy slogans were used to advertise the new fuels, and sponsorship of leading racing drivers helped to publicize the BP brand.

in 1934 and in 1939 a new refinery, jointly owned by Anglo-Persian and Royal Dutch-Shell, came on stream at Haifa.

The opening of the pipeline finally brought Iraq into the ranks of the major oil-exporting nations. It also gave Anglo-Persian a source of export crude oil outside Persia (production from the Naft Khaneh oilfield went entirely for local consumption in Iraq). Anglo-Persian's liftings of Iraqi

50 Route of oil pipeline from Kirkuk to Tripoli and Haifa on the Mediterranean coast, completed in 1934. A new refinery came on stream at Haifa in 1939.

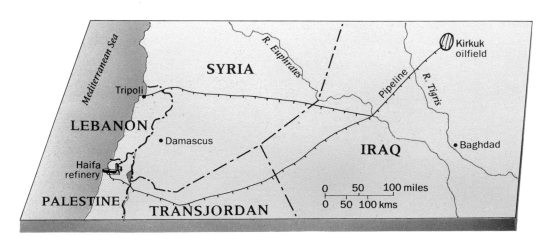

This striking image advertising BP Ethyl was designed by Edward McKnight Kauffer in 1933.

crude were much less than its crude production in Persia. But the huge Kirkuk oilfield had ample capacity for increased production in later years.

Anglo-Persian was also watching developments in other Middle Eastern states. The company was particularly upset about what was happening in Bahrain where, as the company's general manager in Persia and Iraq, Edward Elkington, put it: 'Our hands had been tied by various government departments enabling an independent freebooter to slip in under our noses and that of HMG and commit the Sheikh of Bahrain to granting him a concession.'

The 'freebooter' was Frank Holmes, a New Zealand engineer who had first visited the Middle East in 1918 as a quartermaster in the British Army. Impressed by Anglo-Persian's operations in Persia, Holmes had persuaded King Ibn Saud to grant his company, the Eastern & General Syndicate, an exclusive oil concession for the El Hasa province of Saudi Arabia in 1923 and another for the neutral zone between Saudi Arabia and Kuwait the following year. Holmes also won the oil rights for the small island of Bahrain.

Eastern & General's early exploration programme, however, was unsuccessful and by 1926 Holmes was desperate for money. He attempted to sell his Saudi Arabian concession to Anglo-Persian. The company turned him down. Eventually he sold it to Standard Oil of California (Socal), which had already acquired the oil concession for Bahrain. Socal began drilling at the end of 1931 and oil was first found on 31 May 1932.

The Bahrain discovery concentrated a lot of minds and gave a new impetus to negotiations in Kuwait, whose ruler Sheikh Ahmad wrote to the Colonial Office: 'It was a stab to my heart when I observed the oil work at Bahrain and nothing here.'

The Sheikh added pointedly that he was willing to grant the Kuwaiti concession to Frank Holmes, who by then had been courting Kuwait's ruler for nine years.

Anglo-Persian's interest in the small state at the head of the Persian Gulf, however, dated back to 1911. Negotiations for oil rights had been conducted through the Colonial Office and by 1923 a draft agreement was

Sheikh Ahmad al-Jabir and followers with company representatives at Bahra, Kuwait, 1936. It was not until the discovery of the Burgan oilfield in 1938 that Kuwait's huge potential as an oil-producer was realized.

under discussion, although the company had not pressed its suit. Its survey of prospects near Burgan, 25 miles south of the capital of the small state, had been discouraging. Indeed, until the Bahrain discovery, no oil had been found anywhere on the Arab side of the Gulf. But the grudging acceptance by the UK of an open-door policy towards US investment in the Middle East, and the upheaval in Persia, persuaded Anglo-Persian that it must protect its position in Kuwait by seeking to obtain an oil concession there.

By this time Sheikh Ahmad was thoroughly disillusioned with the company. That did not stop him tirelessly playing it off against Gulf Oil in search of better terms.

In May 1933, the two companies wearied of competing for the concession and formed the Kuwait Oil Company to make a joint bid. But the Sheikh stubbornly refused their combined offer until the new partners acceded to his demands. The oil concession was finally granted in December 1934.

The following March geologists from Anglo-Persian and Gulf arrived in Kuwait. Other staff and equipment followed and in May 1936 the first well was spudded at Bahra, in the presence of the Sheikh. It was abandoned at a depth of 7,950 ft without striking oil. A geophysical survey in the winter of 1936–7 resulted in the selection of a second drilling location in the Burgan area, where the first well drilled brought forth a great gush of oil on the night of 23 February 1938. Further drilling confirmed the enormous size of the Burgan field. The Kuwaiti oil industry had been born.

By then the world economy was emerging from the depths of the Great Depression. By 1934 average US crude prices had crept back up to $1 a

BP and Shell merged their UK marketing operations to form Shell-Mex and BP in 1932. This arrangement lasted until 1976.

Enamel road-sign, 1920s.

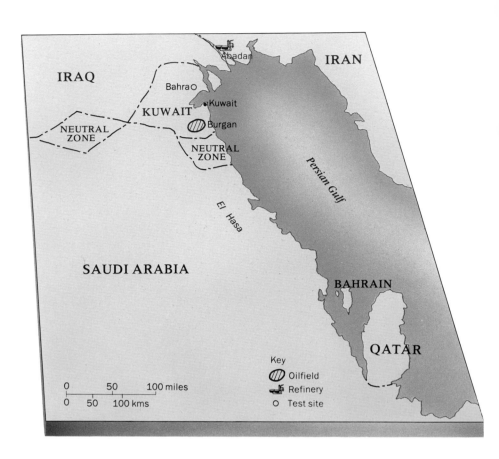

52 Anglo-Persian and Gulf Oil were jointly granted the oil concession in Kuwait in 1934, and discovered the Burgan field in 1938.

A BP Plus pump, 1931.

barrel. Anglo-Persian's profits also revived, rising year on year from 1933 to 1937, when they reached £9.8m. Capital expenditure was increased and by 1936 exceeded the pre-Depression level. With improved profitability, the company was able to raise its dividend.

The rise in profits was not just due to the recovery in prices. Sales volumes rose rapidly, from 117,000 barrels of products a day in 1931 to 209,000 barrels in 1937. The bulk of these sales were fuel oils for merchant vessels and for the Royal Navy, which remained a very large customer. Much, too, was sold in Europe, through the marketing subsidiaries and associates which the company had built up in the 1920s.

By far the largest national market for Anglo-Persian was Britain, where demand for oil products was growing strongly. Although industries such as coal, steel and cotton textiles remained under the shadow of long-term decline, new industries and increased consumer spending in prosperous areas of the country boosted sales of oil products, none more so than petrol. Motoring caught the imagination of a widening public and became more affordable as automobile manufacturers introduced improved production methods and exploited economies of scale to reduce prices of new cars. At the same time, the price of premier-grade petrol, excluding tax, fell from 1s. 1d. (5.4p) a gallon in 1928 to 10d. (4.2p) a gallon a decade later, helping to hold down the rise in the retail price caused by a doubling of excise tax to 9d. (3.7p) a gallon. The number of licensed cars in the UK rose from fewer than a million in 1928 to nearly two million a decade later.

There was also rapid growth in commercial road transport, from local delivery services by laundries, department stores and others to longer-distance haulage which was challenging the railways for freight.

The development of the petrol market was not simply a matter of volume. Improvements in engine design and higher compression ratios called for higher-octane fuel, on which much research was done at BP's Sunbury research centre.

This more potent petrol was promoted by catchy advertising, with the BP and Shell brands continuing to compete after the two parent companies merged their UK marketing operations into Shell-Mex and BP. When tetraethyl lead was introduced as an additive to boost performance in 1931, the new grade was given the name 'BP Plus' and advertised as 'Plus a little something others haven't got'. 'BP Plus' raised the BP brand's place in the petrol rankings, although Sunbury had to deal with complaints that the new grade caused valve sticking and convince the Austin car company that the trouble was due to its engine design, not to the fuel. The use of tetraethyl lead was behind the change in the brand name of BP's premier grade to BP Ethyl in 1934. Witty captions advertised the new grade, and sponsorship of racing drivers such as Captain George Eyston, Henry Segrave and Malcolm Campbell helped to publicize the BP brand.

In spite of product promotion, Shell-Mex and BP's market share was eroded by smaller, low-cost competitors who targeted the most profitable segments of the market. Shell-Mex and BP maintained its share above 40 per cent only by acquiring the Power Petroleum Company and the Dominion Motor Company in 1934.

On mainland Europe, other changes were taking place. After the 'As-Is' Agreement of 1928, Anglo-Persian had agreed to give up its direct marketing interests in Italy in return for an undertaking from Royal Dutch-Shell and Standard Oil (New Jersey) to purchase 20 per cent of their main product requirements for the Italian market from Anglo-Persian. Elsewhere, however, sales expanded. In France, a new refinery was constructed

An early BP road tanker in Switzerland.

Shell-Mex and BP acquired the Dominion Motor Company in 1934.

BP advertising poster shows Captain George Eyston using BP Ethyl to set a new speed record, 1935.

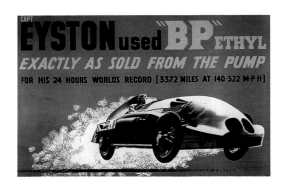

Right A striking advertisement from Germany, 1936.

Above BP's Sunbury research centre started modestly at Meadhurst, a country house near Sunbury-on-Thames, England, in 1917. The centre later moved to a larger site near by and today continues to play a key scientific and engineering role. This picture shows a laboratory at Sunbury in 1937.

Lord Cadman of Silverdale, chairman from 1927 to 1941. He was previously professor of mining at Birmingham University. During his chairmanship, in 1935, the company changed its name from the Anglo-Persian Oil Company to the Anglo-Iranian Oil Company.

at Lavéra in 1931 and in Belgium Anglo-Persian's subsidiary, L'Alliance, purchased Sinclair Petroleum Société Anonyme in 1937, adding 3 per cent to its market share. Most of Anglo-Persian's oil deliveries to Europe were shipped by the British Tanker Company, whose fleet had grown by 1937 to 86 tankers with a combined deadweight of 885,000 tons.

The increase in Anglo-Persian's sales lifted crude oil production and refining in Persia, still the main source of the company's oil supplies. With the royalty now based on tonnage, Anglo-Persian's payments to the Persian government doubled from £1.8m. in 1933 to £3.5m. in 1937. This improvement made for better relations between Anglo-Persian and Riza Shah, who was spending lavishly on the modernization of his country, which he renamed Iran in 1935 on the grounds that the name Persia derived from the province of Pars, the modern Fars, whereas Iran applied to the whole of the 'land of the Aryans'. The company quickly changed its name to the Anglo-Iranian Oil Company.

However, the recovery peaked in 1937. Demand in that year was boosted by a build-up of reserve oil stocks as international rearmament intensified, enabling Anglo-Iranian to increase production in Iran to record levels. By the spring of 1938 the build-up was virtually complete. For 1938 as a whole, Anglo-Iranian's sales were down. The fall in demand meant reduced oil exports from Iran and reduced royalties.

Anglo-Iranian's deputy chairman, William Fraser, tried to explain the market downturn to the Shah, cautioning that 'phenomenal expansion is not a normal expectation'. The Shah was not amused. 'You will of course agree how unpleasant it is for a progressive country like Iran, which must administer its affairs according to a definite programme and cannot relegate its business to chance, nor place its trust upon supernatural assistance, to have to confront such an unexpected issue,' he wrote sternly to Cadman. The chairman explained that world oil consumption had fallen by 50 million barrels, that new oil discoveries had been made nearer to major markets, that US tariff barriers and a ban on imports into Russia excluded the company from 70 per cent of the world's markets, and that improvements in engine design were improving fuel economy.

Riza Shah found his explanations so unacceptable that he felt 'it is better that I should abstain from direct discussion of the problem'. Cadman, who was ill, sent Neville Gass, a senior BP executive, to Tehran. Gass reported that the company was 'definitely in disfavour . . . behind it is the belief that the oil resources of the country should and can be converted into money'. Worried, Cadman wrote to Fraser: 'On full reflection of the whole matter, I am inclined to think we are not on a very sound policy by sticking to the terms of the agreement. We must not forget we are dealing with an abnormal man and an abnormal case.'

As soon as he had recovered, Cadman flew to Tehran, where 'HM finally expressed satisfaction with my explanation.' But, as the war clouds gathered over Europe, Anglo-Iranian was about to face much larger disruptions to its business.

A BP service station in Switzerland, 1930s.

Shell-Mex and BP acquired the Power Petroleum Company in 1934.

A poster advertising Whipsnade Zoo by Clifford and Rosemary Ellis, 1932, also promotes BP Plus.

Chapter Seven

The World at War

Left Lancaster bombers of No. 50 squadron over England at the start of a mission in August 1943. As the struggle for air supremacy intensified, demand for high-octane aviation spirit became acute. Anglo-Iranian's refinery at Abadan played a major role in supplying the Allied air forces.

Oil was even more essential to the armies, navies and air forces which clashed in World War II than it had been in the first. As the conflict spread across the globe, there was hardly a phase or a theatre of the war which left the company untouched.

After Britain declared war on Germany on 3 September 1939, Anglo-Iranian evacuated 900 of its headquarters staff from central London to the research station at Sunbury and to Llandarcy, where office space was provided in the main building, the Llandarcy Institute, the sports pavilion and the bowling-green pavilion. Only 15 people remained to look after Britannic House.

Anglo-Iranian assumed that normal research would cease under the emergency conditions of war and the number of technical staff at Sunbury was reduced sharply. But it soon became apparent that high-octane aviation spirit would be vital to the war effort and that the Sunbury research centre would have to solve the problem of producing high-grade aviation

Right BP tanker with its logo almost concealed by the 'Pool' name. During World War II, oil companies in the UK agreed to pool their petrol deliveries. Features of competition, such as brand names and advertising, were suspended. Petrol was available only in a single rationed grade known as Pool Motor Spirit.

spirit from Iranian crude oil. Technical staff were re-employed and others recruited. Including staff evacuated from London, Sunbury became very overcrowded. Improvisation and temporary accommodation near by enabled the company to function from its temporary headquarters.

Anglo-Iranian also participated in the Petroleum Board, which was in effect a combined distribution agency for the oil companies operating in Britain. The usual features of competition, such as brand names and advertising, were eliminated and all plant and equipment, such as depots and storage tanks, railway wagons and lorries, were pooled. At the same time

By the beginning of World War II Anglo-Iranian was producing crude oil from its small onshore fields in the UK. This 'nodding donkey' was installed at Eakring in Nottinghamshire, 1943.

A statue at Eakring commemorates the contribution which was made by American oilmen to Anglo-Iranian's operations in the UK during the war.

the number of grades of products was greatly reduced. Petrol was available only in a single rationed grade known as Pool Motor Spirit. As the panoply of wartime administration expanded, more and more Anglo-Iranian employees became members of one official committee or another.

In the spring of 1940, western Europe was devastated by German attacks on Denmark, Norway, the Low Countries and France. By the end of May, the Dutch and Belgian forces had surrendered and in June Britain's outlook was made bleaker by the fall of France and Italy's entry into the war on the German side. These events had dramatic effects on Anglo-Iranian's operations. For a start, the Mediterranean was closed to Allied shipping. As a result, Anglo-Iranian's tankers could no longer carry their cargoes of crude oil and products from the Middle East to Europe via the Suez Canal and the Mediterranean. Instead, they had to proceed by the much longer route around Africa by the Cape of Good Hope. As voyages took longer to complete, tanker capacity was insufficient to maintain the pre-war volume of trade.

At first, this did not greatly matter because, with much of continental Europe under German occupation, Anglo-Iranian no longer had access to those markets. But in the second half of 1940, as tanker losses to enemy action mounted, it became necessary to save tanker tonnage by reducing oil liftings from Iran in favour of nearer sources in the Western hemisphere, mainly the USA. Oil loadings for Britain from Iran were stopped and the last cargo of Iranian oil arrived in Britain in August 1941.

Anglo-Iranian's British refineries had already felt the effects of war. Refining in Britain was considered wasteful of tanker tonnage because the refineries themselves used some of the imported oil as fuel. The Grangemouth refinery, which had the additional disadvantage of being on the vulnerable east coast, was shut down in March 1940. The Llandarcy refinery had already been brought almost to a halt on the outbreak of war so its staff could man the factory constructed there to make petrol containers for the armed services. Refining operations gradually restarted on Middle East crude in October 1939, but air raids made it difficult to keep them going. However, the plant was kept running until September 1941, when its crude supplies were exhausted. Operations were suspended until March 1942, when the refinery began making lubricants, using feedstocks supplied from the Western hemisphere.

The war made any supplies of oil valuable. Almost on the eve of the war, Anglo-Iranian had begun to produce crude oil from its small onshore British oilfields at Hardstoft in Derbyshire, Formby in Lancashire, and Eakring in Nottinghamshire. The British government urged Anglo-Iranian to increase its crude production in Britain as a contribution to the war effort. It set a target of about 2,000 barrels a day, a fourfold increase on Anglo-Iranian's existing production. The company achieved the target production rate in September 1942.

It also undertook the manufacture of petrol cans, the erection of fuel storage depots and various projects for the Petroleum Warfare Department, to which company employees were seconded to work on devices such as flame-traps, flame-barrages and flame-throwers. The best-known schemes in which the company was involved went by the acronyms PLUTO and FIDO. The first, standing for Pipeline Under The Ocean, was designed to support the Allied invasion of France in 1944 with oil supplies transported across the English Channel through small-bore pipelines laid on the seabed. The second, standing for Fog Investigation Dispersal

One of the enormous bobbins, known as 'conundrums', which unwound the petrol pipelines under the English Channel in Operation PLUTO, 1944.

Operations, was designed to dissipate fog at airfields so that aircraft could land safely.

In the Middle East, British troops overcame the pro-Axis government of Rashid Ali al-Gaylani in Iraq in 1941 and occupied the country. Iraq Petroleum had cut production heavily because, with the Mediterranean closed to Allied shipping, there was no way of moving Iraqi oil from the pipeline terminals at Tripoli and Haifa. But as Allied troops occupied Iraq, demand for oil there increased sharply. To meet this, throughput at the local refinery was doubled and stabilization units at Kirkuk were converted to produce 70-octane motor fuel. New pipelines were laid for the local distribution, and tin plants for the manufacture of petrol containers were erected at Kirkuk and Mosul. Other work by Iraq Petroleum for the occupying forces included mounting fuel tanks on military vehicles, installing

Picture Post cover, 1943.

German troops advance
through a Soviet oilfield,
the storage tanks having been
set on fire by the retreating
Russians.

lorry- and rail-loading facilities, erecting kerbside pumps and tanks, seconding specialist staff and providing supplies of all kinds.

In 1942 the military command decided that most of the producing wells in the Kirkuk field should be destroyed in case they fell into enemy hands. All but six of the wells were permanently plugged. Similar measures were taken in Kuwait, where wells in the great Burgan field were plugged with cement and most of the materials and equipment removed from the sheikhdom.

Iran was a much bigger worry. After Britain declared war on Germany, Riza Shah declared Iran a neutral country. Despite this, the British government became increasingly concerned about the extent of German influence in Iran. During the 1930s Germany had forged strong trading links with the country. Germany's economic penetration there was accompanied by many German commercial agents and technicians. According to the British Minister in Tehran, Sir Reader Bullard, these devoted particular attention to the military and merchant classes 'with conspicuous success in predisposing them against the United Kingdom and persuading them of the chances of German victory'.

The British cause was not helped by a steep fall in royalties to Iran from Anglo-Iranian. Stringent restrictions on civilian demand in the United Kingdom, coupled with an acute shortage of tanker tonnage and the threat to shipping from the German Navy, meant the company had no option but to cut its crude oil production and refining operations in Iran. In 1938 it had been producing nearly 210,000 barrels of crude oil a day. By 1940 this had fallen to 176,000 barrels and by 1941 it was a mere 135,000 barrels. As the royalty was based on a rate per ton, the drop in production meant lower oil revenues for Iran. Cadman explained the reasons for the cut to the Shah, but made no impression on him. Riza Shah could not understand why oil consumption had diminished. Was firewood being used in England as a substitute? He sent a message to the chairman: 'I hope Lord Cadman is in the best of health. He must understand that the production of oil from Iran must not be less than in 1937.'

The Iranian government warned, too, that if compensation for the reduced royalties could not be arranged, it would 'revise the oil concession fundamentally'. Alarmed, the British government agreed that it would share with the company the cost of additional payments to compensate Iran for shortfalls in income. An extra £1.5m. was paid immediately for 1939, followed by £1.3m. for 1940 and £1.9m. for 1941.

Britain remained deeply concerned about Iran. After the defeat of Rashid Ali in May 1941, it was thought the Germans might try to set up a puppet government there. In June, Hitler invaded the Soviet Union, raising the prospect that German forces might conquer the Caucasus and threaten Iran from the north. In any case, Iran was now a vital route for Allied supplies to the Soviet Union. Britain sent Riza Shah a list of German officers living in Iran under commercial disguises and urged him to arrange for their departure. He refused. Bullard repeated the request on 24 August, but there was no change in Iran's attitude.

The following day two divisions of the British Indian Army entered Iran, one with orders to occupy Khurramshahr (the modern name for Mohammerah) and Abadan and push on to protect the oilfields, and the other to take Kermanshah and join forces with Soviet troops invading Iran from the north. The Iranians offered little real opposition and on 28 August the Shah ordered all resistance to cease. In September, as the Allied

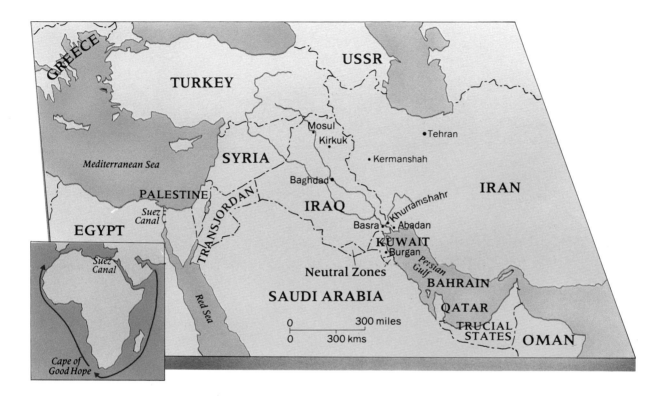

forces moved towards Tehran, Riza Shah abdicated in favour of his son Mohammed, then a few weeks short of his 22nd birthday.

The Allied invasion was formalized in January 1942 by a 'tripartite pact' which ceded to Britain and the Soviet Union the right to keep armed forces in Iran for the duration of the war. They were given rights of passage for troops and supplies and unrestricted use of Iranian railways, roads, rivers, ports, airports, telephones and pipelines. In return, the Allies guaranteed the sovereignty and independence of Iran and promised to defend the country against the Axis powers. The pact expressly stipulated that the Allied presence was not a military occupation. Nobody was fooled, Anglo-Iranian least of all. Although three of its staff had been killed by 'friendly fire' when the invading troops engaged the Iranian garrison at Abadan, relations with the military command rapidly became extremely close. The company's barges were used to transport railway engines, tanks and other vehicles for the Soviet Union up the River Karun. Abadan doubled its production of petrol cans to supply the armed forces and asphalt was supplied in large quantities for military roads and depots. Of

Iran was of great strategic importance to the Allies. Its oilfields kept working but, after the closure of the Mediterranean to Allied ships and enemy action at sea, Anglo-Iranian's oil tankers had to make long, hazardous journeys around the Cape of Good Hope to reach Europe. After the enemy seized oilfields in Burma and the Dutch East Indies, Abadan started to supply the Allied forces in the Pacific and the Far East too.

course, the company provided the Allies with all their local fuel requirements, soon to become much greater.

On 7 December 1941 the Japanese bombed Pearl Harbor, turning the whole of the Pacific and the Far East into one gigantic battleground. The shortest haul for oil to this new theatre of war was from Burma and the Dutch East Indies, but these fuel sources were soon seized by the enemy. At the top of the Persian Gulf, however, Abadan, the largest refinery in the world, idled at half capacity.

Production from the company's oilfields was increased dramatically to meet the new demand from the East. From 135,000 barrels a day in 1941 it leaped to 192,000 the following year, then 272,000 in 1944 and 345,000 barrels a day in 1945. The company also began pumping gas condensate from its gas find at Pazanun, another of Professor de Böckh's recommendations, half-way between Agha Jari and Gach Saran. The condensate contained isobutane, an essential ingredient in high-octane aviation spirit. As the struggle for air supremacy intensified, demand for this most highly refined oil product became desperate. The company had already invented a process called alkylation for making 100-octane aviation fuel at its Sunbury research station in England. But producing it on a large-scale at Abadan required huge superfractionating towers. Three ships carrying the material to build these were sunk before the final consignment reached Iran

The Japanese bombed Pearl Harbor on 7 December 1941, extending the war to the whole of the Pacific and the Far East.

from the USA in the spring of 1942. It took another 15 months before the first tower was in operation. By May 1945, however, Abadan was producing high-octane fuel at a rate of 20,000 barrels a day.

The enormous increase in output, not to mention the development of new processes for aviation fuel, stretched the resources of the company in Iran to the limit. As the war dragged on, the local staff had to resort to ever-greater ingenuity to keep everything going.

The Control Instrument section in Abadan, for example, manufactured surgical instruments, made height computers and automatic pilot lights for the refinery's anti-aircraft batteries, designed a new steering unit for a tanker and repaired everyone's clocks and watches. It produced police badges, rubber stamps, pens, pins, springs, sprockets, padlocks, wall safes, petrol lighters, reconditioned golf and squash balls, and made sirens out of empty shell cases. The refinery also turned out several hundred thousand oil drums a year, the work done mostly by Indian employees convicted of serious crimes.

Masjid-i-Suleiman's scrapheap, estimated to contain 15,000 tons of steel accumulated over 30 years, was picked over by senior engineers, like tramps searching rubbish bins for returnable soft-drinks cans. Every possible piece of metal was extracted and given a second life.

Even greater challenges were to keep everyone fed and to control the price of food. There was a serious shortage of wheat as early as 1941 and a year later the queues in the Abadan bazaar were nearly a mile long. Sydney Taylor was sent out from London to organize supplies and rationing. He began with a census which revealed that the population of Abadan was 125,000, with another 80,000 living at the oilfields.

The Ministry of Food printed ration books, and tankers brought rice, flour, tea and sugar from India, Australia and anywhere else supplies could be found, as well as second-hand clothing from the UK. The company distributed them from its own shops, mostly square courtyards entered through turnstiles. Taylor established a dairy herd, founded a local fishing industry and painstakingly created a 15-acre farm to grow fresh vegetables. After extracting a hundred tons of salt from every acre, he had to fertilize the barren soil with ash from Abadan's incinerators. Every effort, however, brought only partial relief, with supplies even for the British staff at least as stringent and monotonous as in the UK. They perhaps reached rock bottom late in 1943 when one of the remaining wives planted her ration of dehydrated mutton in the belief that it was nasturtium seeds.

Even so, compared with most of Iran, the company's operations were an island of plenty and Abadan 'became the Mecca of the starving population of Persia'. Near-famine in the surrounding countryside contributed to an outbreak of smallpox in 1942. Mass vaccinations of all employees were carried out by the company's medical staff. A typhus epidemic affected more than 1,000 employees a year later. Disinfection centres and more vaccinations helped bring this disease under control.

Another problem was a gradual erosion of skilled manpower. The company's operations in Iran were classified as essential undertakings and

Pipelines al Agha Jari leading to the Abadan refinery.

63

A British soldier guards oil pipelines in Iran.

Above A British convoy, on its way to Russia, under massive air attack, 1942. (Painting by Charles Pears.) The British Merchant Navy, including the Anglo-Iranian tanker fleet, suffered heavy casualties while carrying essential supplies to Britain and other areas of the conflict.

Anglo-Iranian tanker losses during World War II. In all, 44 vessels were sunk, with the loss of 657 lives.

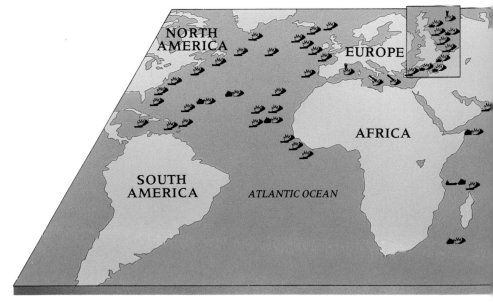

British subjects were not allowed to leave their jobs without the permission of the British Ambassador. Although the number of Iranian labourers rose dramatically, from fewer than 25,000 in the middle of 1941 to more than 60,000 in 1945, many skilled employees left to work for the British and American forces. As the company's technical director James 'J J' Jameson admitted in 1944, the advances in training Iranians made before the war had, by its end, been 'virtually lost'.

That, however, was less grievous than the loss of tankers. By the end of the war 44 of Anglo-Iranian's tankers had been sunk, nearly half the pre-war fleet. In a dreadful tally, 657 crew lost their lives, and 260 were taken prisoner of war. But by the end of 1945 the fleet was back up to 82 vessels, totalling nearly 900,000 tons.

With production at record levels, profits, too, were higher than they had ever been, rising from £7.4m. in 1939 to £23.4m. in 1945. This, though, was before tax. Excess profits tax in 1945 wiped out all the gain compared with 1939. But the company emerged from the war with negligible debt and a healthy cash flow, continuing to practise the financial self-reliance which had become its habit in the pre-war decade.

The few survivors of a British vessel sunk by torpedo in 1942. The smoke on the horizon marks their sinking ship.

ASIA

AN OCEAN

KEY

Torpedoed
Mined
Bombed
Aerial torpedoed
Sunk by raider
Captured by raider

AUSTRALIA

Chapter Eight

A Rather Long-Term Job

A modern photograph of the company's refinery at Lavéra, France. First built in 1931, the refinery was refurbished after World War II in response to growing demand for oil throughout Europe. By 1950, the company held 13 per cent of the European market for oil products compared with only 8 per cent in 1938.

The defeat of Germany and Japan, the devastation of France and Italy, and the exhaustion of Britain changed for ever the political environment in which Anglo-Iranian operated.

The post-war economic environment presented the company with substantial opportunities to expand its operations and increase its share of oil markets. Coal shortages accelerated the long-term switch from coal to oil, and trends in international oil supply and demand created new openings, especially in Europe, which before the war had been supplied largely from the USA. After the war the USA became a net importer and Europe turned increasingly to the Middle East for its oil. Anglo-Iranian, with its huge stake in the region, was well placed to supply its needs. It also had the advantage of being in the sterling area. This gave Anglo-Iranian a competitive advantage over American oil companies, which sold oil for dollars, a currency in very short supply outside the Western hemisphere.

However, because the British government owned a majority shareholding in Anglo-Iranian, the company continued to be seen widely as an arm of the British government. This had drawbacks in an age when Britain's imperial power was waning and nationalism in the Middle East and elsewhere was on the rise.

It was fortunate that demand was growing fast, as the company had a vast upstream capacity from its Middle Eastern interests. In Iraq, plans to increase the pipeline capacity from Kirkuk to the Mediterranean were revived after the end of the war and in 1946 the Iraq Petroleum Company began construction of new pipelines parallel to the ones completed in 1934. Construction of the southern line to Haifa was nearing completion by early 1948. But just when the new pipeline was due to come on stream, it became a pawn in Middle Eastern politics.

On 14 May 1948, the British mandate over Palestine was terminated and the last British forces were withdrawn from the country. The same day, the Jews in Palestine proclaimed the establishment of the state of Israel, to which President Truman extended US recognition only a few hours later. In retaliation, Arab armies, including Iraqi forces, entered Palestine only to suffer military defeat.

By then the Iraqi government had stopped the flow of oil through the pipeline linking Kirkuk with Haifa, now in Israel. The original 1934 pipeline was closed, the new pipeline was abandoned and the Haifa refinery, jointly owned by Anglo-Iranian and Royal Dutch-Shell, was starved of crude supplies. Although some cargoes of Venezuelan crude reached the plant from 1949, they only filled a fraction of its refining capacity. Meanwhile, production from the Kirkuk field was cut back because of the

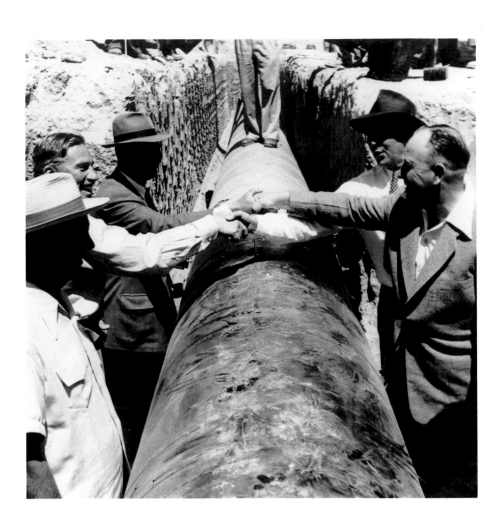

68 Engineers shake hands to mark the final stages of the new pipeline linking the Kirkuk field in Iraq to Banias in Syria, 1952.

British soldiers patrol Jerusalem in the late 1930s. The British left Palestine on 14 May 1948. On the same day the Palestinian Jews proclaimed the state of Israel. Their Arab neighbours were incensed. The Iraqis blocked the oil pipeline to Haifa (now in Israel). For the first time in the Middle East, an oil embargo was being used as a weapon in an international dispute.

pipeline closure. For the first time in the Middle East, an oil embargo was being used as a weapon in an international dispute. It took a new pipeline along the northern route to Tripoli, completed in 1951, and a much larger new line linking Kirkuk to a new terminal at Banias in Syria in 1952 to restore Iraq's exports.

Meanwhile, Iraq Petroleum developed new oilfields at Zubair and Ain Zala in Iraq. In Qatar it brought the Dukhan oilfield on stream in 1949. As a result of these developments, Anglo-Iranian's liftings of crude from Iraq and Qatar rose to 43,000 barrels a day by 1950.

In Kuwait, the development of the great Burgan field had been delayed by the war. But in the last few months of 1945 staff and materials were reassembled, buildings refurbished, the wells cleaned out and the provision of facilities such as gathering lines, gas separators, storage tanks and pipelines put in hand. A temporary marine loading terminal was constructed at Fahahil and the first cargo of Kuwaiti crude was exported on 30 June 1946. Production increased extremely fast and by 1950 Anglo-Iranian was lifting nearly 150,000 barrels a day of Kuwaiti crude.

Iran, however, remained by far Anglo-Iranian's largest production and refining centre. The Abadan refinery was the largest in the world and Iran was still the leading oil producer in the Middle East, although the explosive growth in production from nearby Arab states, led by Saudi Arabia, threatened its supremacy. Anglo-Iranian could not afford to allow Iran to fall behind. After the war, Sir William Fraser, who had succeeded Cadman as chairman in 1941, personally determined that maintaining Iran's position in the oil industry should be the core of Anglo-Iranian's strategy. This required a great expansion of the company's Iranian operations. The numbers employed by the company in Iran rose to 83,000 in 1949, while capital was poured into the country in amounts that would have been unimaginable before the war. Production increased substantially from the fields at Gach Saran, Naft Safid and Lali and spectacularly from Agha Jari. By 1950, Iran's output had risen to 650,000 barrels a day.

With oil pouring out of Iran, Kuwait and Iraq, plus continued small-scale production from onshore fields in Britain, Anglo-Iranian had plenty of crude with which to meet the growing demand for oil. But the company's capacity upstream was not matched by the much smaller downstream facilities that Anglo-Iranian had built up before the war. This, Fraser recognized, was 'a very major problem'. His first idea to solve it was to extend the company's joint marketing with Royal Dutch-Shell across a much greater territory, in fact most of the world. Shell rejected his proposals and Anglo-Iranian was forced to begin building up its own marketing organization, which Fraser admitted in 1945 was 'a rather long-term job'. Over the next five years Anglo-Iranian's marketers made substantial progress in expanding its sales outlets. At the same time, the company concentrated new refining capacity in Europe, close to its main markets.

In Britain, where the company sold its refined products through Shell-Mex and BP, many of the wartime controls on the oil industry were kept in force by Clement Attlee's post-war Labour government. The Petroleum Board was not dissolved until 1948 and petrol rationing continued until 1950. A decade had elapsed with almost no competition in the British market. But sales still increased, especially of fuel oil as the chronic shortage of coal encouraged consumers to switch to oil. The Llandarcy and Grangemouth refineries were expanded and construction of a new refinery on the Isle of Grain in the Thames estuary began in 1950.

Although Britain remained the largest market for the company's products, it was not the fastest-growing. In Australasia, sales were boosted by entry into the New Zealand market in 1949 in partnership with the government. In Europe Anglo-Iranian achieved dynamic growth in business through its various local subsidiaries and associates.

The refinery at Lavéra, near Marseilles, in France was refurbished and a new refinery at Dunkirk was brought on stream, replacing the war-damaged plant at Courchelettes. In Germany, Anglo-Iranian acquired a refinery at Hamburg and boosted its market share by buying a small distribution organization named Runo-Everth. In Belgium, it reached agreement with Petrofina to share in the construction of a new refinery at Antwerp. In the Netherlands, the acquisition of independent distributors Nohaka, Tankopslag and Fanto helped to increase business. In Switzerland, the company bought Noba, a distribution company. In

Sheikh Ahmad al-Jabir inaugurates the first cargo of crude oil for export at Fahahil, Kuwait, 30 June 1946.

Anglo-Iranian's chairman, Sir William Fraser (left), with the Shah of Iran during the latter's visit to Sunbury, 1948. After the war Anglo-Iranian invested heavily in Iran, and oil production increased rapidly.

70 Lunch-break for workers on a
pipeline in Iraq, 1950.

In the UK, the Petroleum Board
was not dissolved until 1948
and petrol rationing continued
until 1950. These two cartoons
mark the end of 'Pool' motor
spirit which was introduced at
the start of World War II.

Luncheon to celebrate the passing of 'POOL'

That's Pool—That was!

Greece, it acquired the distributing organization of Steaua (Agencies)
Limited, while in Scandinavia, local subsidiaries and associates in Sweden,
Denmark, and Norway achieved exceptionally rapid growth in sales. In
Italy, under an agreement with AGIP, the state oil company, Anglo-Iranian
acquired a 49-per-cent stake in the Marghera refinery at Venice with the
right to supply the refinery with crude. Products from the refinery were
marketed through AGIP.

Construction work at the Isle
of Grain refinery in Kent,
England, 1952.

Shortly before the death of her husband, King George VI, Queen Elizabeth tours the company's housing estate on a visit to Grangemouth refinery in Scotland in 1952.

Service station at Horsham in Victoria, Australia, 1950. The 'COR' symbol of Commonwealth Oil Refineries, jointly owned by Anglo-Iranian and the Australian government, was a familiar sight in the country.

By 1950 Anglo-Iranian's marketing network in mainland Europe held 13 per cent of the market for oil products, compared with only 8 per cent in 1938. Despite this effort, the company's marketing outlets were still not nearly big enough to take all its production. A growing proportion of Anglo-Iranian's output was sold as crude or products to other oil companies. By 1950, 46 per cent of Anglo-Iranian's sales were to other refiners and marketers. The company had no alternative. It could not reduce output without jeopardizing its position in Iran, which in any case looked far from secure.

Chapter Nine

Iran: Departure and Return

It is difficult to pinpoint the moment at which nationalization of the Iranian oil industry became inevitable. But it was probably the afternoon of 7 March 1951, when General Ali Razmara was shot dead in the courtyard of the Soltaneh mosque in Tehran by Abdullah Rastiga, a member of a Muslim sect calling itself Fida'iyan-i Islam, 'those who are prepared to die for Islam'.

Razmara, who had crushed a tentative communist separatist movement in the north of Iran after the Soviet troops had left in 1946, was the nearest that Iran had to a military strong man, at a time when the young Shah Mohammed had yet to assert his authority. Razmara had been appointed Prime Minister in the middle of 1950 following the fall of Ali Mansur, the last in a long line of hapless politicians struggling to reconcile the role of the company with the rampant nationalism of both the left and right. Mansur had, in fact, accepted a supplemental agreement between the government and the company which had been signed a year earlier. This raised the royalty rate from 4s. (20p) to 6s. (30p) a ton and increased the total amount payable for 1948 and 1949 to £18m. and £22m. respectively, compared with the £9m. and £13m. due under the 1933 agreement. A one-off payment of £5m. was also promised when the new agreement came into force.

That the company was prepared to offer such improved terms was a measure of the pressures upon it. There was increasing unhappiness in Iran about the slow 'Iranianization' of the workforce. The government was also keenly aware, as were its Arab neighbours, that a new petroleum law based on the principle of a '50–50' split between the state and the oil companies operating within its borders had been passed in Venezuela as long ago as 1943. Anglo-Iranian had firmly rejected suggestions that Iran should have 50 per cent of its earnings, pointing out that much of these came from operations outside the country.

It had no answer to another Iranian grievance, that for the previous 15 years the British government had been taking a larger and larger share of the company's earnings in UK tax. In 1935 the company had paid the Iranian government £2.2m. in tax and royalties, more than five times its British tax bill. In 1940, however, British tax equalled Iran's oil income of £4m.; by 1943 it was three times as much at £12m.; in 1948 it was £18m. against £9m.; and in 1950 it leaped to an extortionate £36m. The amazing rise in the UK's take arose from excess profits taxes imposed during the war and continued by the Labour government. The socialists also introduced voluntary dividend restraint which the company, half-owned by the state, could not circumvent. William Fraser's complaints on Iran's behalf

Mosque, Isfahan, Iran.

Mohammed Musaddiq was instrumental in the nationalization of Anglo-Iranian's interests in Iran.

Iranian cartoon showing Ernest Northcroft, the company's chief representative in Iran from 1945 to 1951, playing the Iranian children's game, 'The wolf and the cattle'. The cartoon caption starts:
Northcroft: 'I am the Lord and carry away the oil.'
Iranian shepherd: 'I am the shepherd; I will not allow it.'
Northcroft: 'My pounds are more valuable.'
Shepherd: 'My oil is more delicious.'

were sympathetically heard by the Foreign Secretary, Ernest Bevin, but did not move the Chancellor of the Exchequer, Stafford Cripps.

The supplemental agreement was first presented to the Majlis for ratification a few days before the end of the Iranian parliament's summer session in 1949. The opponents of the agreement filibustered until the parliamentary session ended and it was nearly a year before the agreement was resubmitted. By that time a new National Party had been formed under the leadership of Mohammed Musaddiq.

Born in about 1882, Musaddiq was related to the previous royal family through his mother. Now nearly 70, he accused the company of paying inadequate royalties, avoiding local taxes, refusing to train Iranian personnel, obtaining the 1933 concession by force, interfering in national politics and depriving the country of its full sovereignty. He called instead for nationalization. Ali Mansur avoided a vote by setting up a special

committee headed by Musaddiq to report to the Majlis on the agreement and hastily resigned as Prime Minister. His successor, General Razmara, tried to persuade Anglo-Iranian to advance his government £25m. in return for a guarantee that the supplemental agreement would be passed. By November this request was down to £8m., but by then it was clear that Musaddiq's oil committee would not approve the agreement on any terms. Its chances became even worse when, on the last day of 1950, Saudi Arabia signed a 50–50 profit-sharing deal with Aramco, the consortium of US companies exploiting the prolific Saudi oil discoveries made in 1938.

Razmara pleaded with the non-National Front members of the oil committee to resist Musaddiq's calls for nationalization. He read the committee reports from Iranian experts which said that nationalization was impractical for technical, political, financial and legal reasons. Musaddiq's supporters claimed the experts had been bribed by the British. On 5 March 1951, Razmara held a press conference to announce that action on the oil question which ignored expert advice would be treason. Two days later he was assassinated. His murder swept away the last vestiges of government resistance to a state take-over. Musaddiq's committee unanimously recommended nationalization the day after Razmara's death and the Majlis accepted its proposals a week later. At the end of April 1951 the Shah signed a nine-point law to implement the nationalization of Iran's oil industry. The end-game had begun.

Musaddiq, who had become Prime Minister on 28 April, played the Iranian hand. 'We shall have to watch him carefully,' judged Sir Francis Shepherd, the British Ambassador in Tehran. 'He is rather tall but has short and bandy legs so that he shambles like a bear, a trait which is generally associated with considerable physical strength. He looks rather like a cab-horse and is slightly deaf so that he listens with a strained but otherwise expressionless look on his face.' Shepherd added: 'He gives the impression of being impervious to argument.'

The subtle Iranian faced a divided team. The British attitude was predictable. Herbert Morrison, who had become Foreign Secretary, told the Iranian Ambassador in London that the UK government did not accept his country's unilateral action and James Callaghan, as Parliamentary Secretary to the Admiralty, revealed that parachutists had been stationed in Cyprus and that the Navy was deploying ships in the Gulf to take 'any action that the situation might demand'. The Cabinet considered a plan for military intervention which argued that the oilfields were too remote but that Abadan could be captured and held by force. 'If Persia were allowed to get away with it, Egypt and other Middle Eastern countries would be encouraged to think they could try things on,' speculated Emmanuel Shinwell, Minister for Defence. 'The next thing might be an attempt to nationalize the Suez Canal.'

Against the atavistic urge to act had to be set the risk to British lives, the danger of hostages being taken and the certainty that the UK would be condemned all over the world for old-fashioned imperialism. The USA was particularly opposed to armed intervention, not because it objected to

Sir William Fraser, later Lord Strathalmond, was chairman for 15 years, from 1941 to 1956. He steered Anglo-Iranian through the war and the Iranian crisis, and presided over its change of name to British Petroleum in 1954.

Air BP fuelling at Baghdad, Iraq, early 1950s.

Basil Jackson (front), Anglo-Iranian's deputy chairman, returns from Tehran after unsuccessful negotiations with Mohammed Musaddiq in June 1951. At the back is Neville Gass who became chairman in 1957.

Iranians pull down the sign from Anglo-Iranian's information office in Tehran, June 1951.

gunboat diplomacy but because it feared Iran would fall under Soviet domination if it failed. America was deeply worried by the prospect of the Soviet empire seizing control of Middle Eastern oil, on which, if it was honest, it had its own designs.

So the UK tamely informed Iran that unless the company's request for arbitration under the terms of the 1933 agreement was accepted, the British government would bring a complaint before the International Court of Justice at The Hague. Musaddiq replied that nationalization was an exercise of Iran's sovereign rights. The British and US ambassadors went to see him. The American remarked on the unemployment and distress that would be caused if the oil operations came to a halt. 'So much the worse for us,' Iran's Prime Minister said.

Basil Jackson, Anglo-Iranian's deputy chairman, travelled to Tehran to try his hand at resolving the dispute. He had no greater success. Nor did Averell Harriman, the US mediator dispatched by Secretary of State, Dean Acheson. Harriman cabled Acheson after one of many meetings with Musaddiq: 'In his dream world, the simple passage of legislation nationalizing the oil industry creates profitable business and everyone is expected to help Iran on the terms he lays down.' Richard Stokes, a socialist millionaire sent by Britain to Tehran with Sir Donald Fergusson of the Ministry of Fuel and Power, fared no better at negotiating a settlement.

In the meantime, Anglo-Iranian's British staff struggled to keep the company's operations in Iran going. Early in June, 25 Iranian officials arrived in Khurramshahr and designated the company's main building there as the 'office of the provisional board of directors come to nationalize oil'. A band played the national anthem, a sheep was sacrificed and Eric Drake, the general manager, discovered his office barred by a soldier with a fixed bayonet. Jackson instructed him to keep his job as long as possible, but Drake found himself in increasing difficulty. Company signs were being pulled down and offices invaded.

The company began evacuating women and children. By the third week in June, only 160 were left. Dealers from the bazaars swooped on abandoned possessions. The oilmen, however, clung to their Persian carpets. The printing press was commandeered to print receipts stating that tanker cargoes were received from the National Iranian Oil Company (NIOC). Drake was accused of sabotage for failing to authorize these receipts, a charge bearing the death penalty under a bill introduced to the Majlis only two days earlier. On the orders of the British Ambassador, he slipped across the river to Basra in Iraq. The rest of the expatriate staff unanimously refused an offer of employment with the NIOC. The USA had already stated that US technicians would not help run the Iranian oil industry and other countries had followed. The sabotage bill was quietly withdrawn.

The British government decided to pull out all tankers until the Iranians changed their minds about the receipts, and Herbert Morrison broadcast to the British staff that 'the refinery and field operations may have to be closed down, at any rate for the present.'

On 5 July, the International Court issued an interim order instructing

Iran to return managerial control to the company. Instead, Iran withdrew its earlier acceptance of the Court's jurisdiction. By the end of September, the Harriman and Stokes missions had both failed, as had British efforts

Anglo-Iranian's expulsion from Abadan pushes the detonation of a Russian atom bomb out of the headlines in British newspapers.

British staff dependants return to England from Iran, June 1951.

to persuade the Shah to dismiss Musaddiq. Iranian troops occupied Abadan and the government set a deadline for the company's British employees to leave the country. The remaining staff gathered in the Gymkhana Club and on 3 and 4 October boarded the Royal Navy cruiser HMS *Mauritius*. After more than 50 years, the company was out of Iran.

Sir William Fraser took the news badly. His bony brow tightened over his long nose, almost a match for Musaddiq's, and his small mouth pursed implacably under his toothbrush moustache. Fraser had been 'terribly flummoxed' by Iranian nationalization, Eric Drake revealed later, and he rejected any suggestion of an agreement which neither restored the *status quo* nor gave the company substantial compensation.

'If Musaddiq is allowed to get away with this monstrous performance it will have the most disastrous effect on other countries,' Neville Gass argued on the company's behalf at a working party set up by the British government to keep developments in Iran under review. 'Other Musaddiqs will arise and what will be left of the fabric of the oil industry to which the Americans profess to attach so much importance?' It was an argument that carried a great deal of weight with the other oil companies operating in the

Middle East, which firmly refused to step into the breach caused by Anglo-Iranian's expulsion. They were also deterred by the company's public warning that it would take whatever action necessary to protect its rights if any organization or individual tried to purchase Iranian oil from the Iranian government. Within weeks Iran's oil exports had fallen to a trickle.

Gass's fears seemed to have less effect on the politicians. In Britain, Fraser was widely disliked by senior civil servants, who thought him narrow-minded and lacking in political insight and urged his removal. George McGhee, US Assistant Secretary of State for Near Eastern affairs, also found him 'obdurate and inflexible'. McGhee was much more sympathetic towards Musaddiq, who enjoyed a brief celebrity when he arrived in America three weeks after the company had been driven from Iran to argue his country's case before the United Nations. After lunch with President Truman, Musaddiq, pleading ill-health, checked into the presidential suite at the Walter Reed hospital, where he held court in pyjamas. 'Everyone petted and took care of him,' wrote Dean Acheson, the US Secretary of State. Acheson was another who thought the company showed 'unusual and persistent stupidity' in its rejection of any compromise. He wrote of Musaddiq later: 'We were, perhaps, slow in realising that he was essentially a rich, reactionary, feudal-minded Persian inspired by a fanatical hatred of the British and a desire to expel them and all their works from the country regardless of cost.'

The company's position was, however, strengthened by the return of Winston Churchill as Prime Minister following the defeat of Labour in the British general election in October 1951. 'I think we should be stubborn even if the temperature rises somewhat for a while,' he told his new Foreign Secretary, Anthony Eden. Truman begged Churchill to accept the validity of Iran's nationalization of its oil industry. 'If Iran goes down the communist drain, it will be little satisfaction to any of us that legal positions were defended to the last,' he wrote. Gradually even the Americans despaired of reaching any agreement with Musaddiq, who was becoming increasingly autocratic and irrational. He survived an attempt by the Shah to replace him at the same time as the International Court ruled that it had no jurisdiction over the oil dispute. George Middleton, the British representative in Tehran, reported that Musaddiq was 'riding the crest of a wave of popular feeling and success'.

Meanwhile Iran, its oil exports blocked, had received no oil revenues for nearly two years and law and order were collapsing. The USA became convinced that Musaddiq would overthrow the Shah, only to be ousted himself by a communist uprising. Churchill lost patience. 'I do not myself see,' he wrote to Truman, 'why two good men asking only what is right and just should not gang up against a third who is doing wrong.' The comment inspired the USA's Central Intelligence Agency to support a coup against Musaddiq in August 1953. At first the coup appeared to have failed and the Shah fled to Baghdad. But key sections of the army rallied to his support and within a week Musaddiq had fallen from power. His overthrow, however, did not mean a return to the 'good old days' before the

Winston Churchill and Harry Truman in conversation. President Truman had begged Churchill to accept the nationalization of Iranian oil.

Sir Neville Gass was chairman from 1957 to 1960. He played an important part in the negotiations to solve the Iranian crisis in the early 1950s.

Abadan refinery, with housing estate in foreground,1951. By then, the company had been involved in Iran for nearly half a century, and it was a great blow to have to leave.

79

company was driven out of Iran. Nationalist feelings still ran high and in any case the Shah and his new government were just as keen to keep control of their country's oil industry – or at least its income. If Anglo-Iranian was to regain even part of its old position, a compromise was needed.

With reluctance, Eden agreed that Herbert Hoover jun. should act as an intermediary. Hoover met Gass and Jackson in Amsterdam, where they told him: 'Having been the party most hurt, we should like to play if possible the biggest part in operating the oil industry in Persia and in disposing of Persian oil.' But in Tehran General Fazlollah Zahedi, the Shah's new Prime Minister, made it clear that his government would not accept the company's return to Iran in sole charge of the oil industry. Fraser was persuaded by Hoover that only a consortium of oil companies would be acceptable. Ungraciously, Anglo-Iranian's chairman invited Royal Dutch-Shell, the five US majors operating in the Middle East – Standard Oil (New Jersey), Standard Oil of New York, Socal, Texaco and Gulf – and Compagnie Française des Pétroles, to talks of a 'hypothetical nature' on the formation of a consortium. Four months of bargaining ended with agreement that Anglo-Iranian should have 40 per cent, Royal Dutch-Shell 14 per cent, the five US companies 8 per cent each and the French company 6 per cent in a new consortium called Iranian Oil Participants (IOP). Another six months were to elapse before Iran could be persuaded to accept the new partnership's proposals, which included a 25-year contract to manage the oilfields and refineries and a 50–50 profit split between Iran and IOP.

The new terms finally received the Shah's assent and on 29 October 1954 the Anglo-Iranian tanker *British Advocate* berthed at Abadan to load the first cargo of oil produced by the consortium. The Iranian oil industry was back in business.

Fraser's intransigence had taken the negotiations to the brink. But he had won the company £25m. in compensation from the Iranian government and £32m. from its new partners, as well as £182m. from a royalty of 10 cents a barrel on future oil exports through Iranian Oil Participants. 'It was a wonderful deal for Fraser, the best deal Willie Fraser ever made,' John Loudon of Royal Dutch-Shell said afterwards. 'After all, Anglo-Iranian actually had nothing to sell. It had already been nationalized.'

Persian carpets were prized souvenirs for many staff evacuated in 1951.

Chapter Ten

Transformation and Growth

Left A Ferrari and a Brabham at the 1966 Belgian Grand Prix. In the 1950s and 1960s, the BP logo was a familiar sight at motor-racing circuits.

The great shift in the company's fortunes was acknowledged in December 1954 by the change of its name to British Petroleum. Although the company still had a big stake in Iran, thanks to its 40-per-cent interest in the consortium, it was no longer the owner and sole operator of the oil industry it had built up in that country. The decision also reflected the transformation of its position outside Iran.

While BP's operations in Iran were at a standstill between 1951 and 1954, liftings of crude from its other sources of supply in Kuwait, Iraq and Qatar had been dramatically increased. To make good the loss of refined products from Abadan, its other refineries, mainly in Europe, raised their throughputs to the maximum. The new Isle of Grain refinery came on stream in the UK and new refineries were constructed at Aden at the southern end of the Red Sea and Kwinana in Australia. These actions were supplemented by purchases of crude and refined products from other oil companies and by chartering additional tankers to cope with the disruption to shipping patterns. Some business was lost, but the company managed to continue supplying its most valued customers and hold on to its

Right Supplying fuel oil to the *Port Chalmers* in New Zealand, 1968. The company's marine bunkering activities grew rapidly in both Australia and New Zealand during the 1960s.

retail market share. Admittedly, profits fell back for three years, but in 1954 they reached a new record and in 1955 exceeded £100m. pre-tax for the first time. The result was a consolation to Fraser in his last year as chairman. In spring 1956, newly ennobled as Baron Strathalmond of Pumpherston, he retired and was succeeded by Basil Jackson.

However, the nationalization crisis in Iran had brought home to BP the risk of depending on one, or even two, big upstream sources. In the past,

Workmen change the plaque at the company's headquarters at Britannic House, London, December 1954.

Ill-health forced Basil Jackson, who became chairman in 1956, to retire after less than a year in office. Jackson had been appointed to the board in 1948, after spending much of his career as the company's representative in the USA.

Right In March 1958, BP chairman Sir Neville Gass (centre) meets the then ruler of Abu Dhabi, Sheikh Shakbut (on Gass's right), and his brother Sheikh Zayed bin Sultan Al Nahyan, who succeeded him as ruler in 1966 and became president of the United Arab Emirates on its formation in 1971. On Gass's left is Tim Hillyard, BP's first representative in Abu Dhabi.

exploration outside Iran had not been a priority. Suddenly it assumed a new relevance, especially when Colonel Gamal Abdul Nasser nationalized the Suez Canal in July 1956. The closure of the canal and the cutting by Syria of the oil pipeline from Iraq to the Mediterranean exposed Europe's vulnerability to interruptions in the supply of Middle Eastern oil. The time taken to ship oil via the Cape of Good Hope reduced BP's supplies to Europe in the four months from November 1956 to February 1957 by 140 million barrels. The company also lost its interest in Anglo-Egyptian Oilfields, which Nasser sequestered.

The political fragility of the Middle East was underlined by a coup in Iraq in 1958, which saw the king who had been installed by the British beheaded by his own troops, his heir shot and mutilated, and his pro-Western Prime Minister lynched. The new government tried to wring large concessions from Iraq Petroleum. The bloody events passed all but unmentioned in the annual statement to shareholders by Neville Gass, who had succeeded Jackson as chairman when the latter had retired, seriously ill, after less than a year in office. But they fuelled BP's desire to find reserves of oil in more stable parts of the world.

Not all the areas chosen for exploration proved to have oil. Malta, for example, was a write-off. Papua New Guinea, where the company had been exploring for years, remained stubbornly unproductive, as did drilling for gas in Australia. BP's minority investment in Trinidad's Gulf of Paria oilfield promised little and exploration in the Rockies and the Gulf of Alaska found nothing, although Triad Oil, in which BP held a majority shareholding, did increase its modest reserves in western Canada. In contrast, the joint programme with Shell in Nigeria, begun in 1938, was rewarded in 1956 with a sizeable discovery. A decision to drill the shallow waters off Abu Dhabi in partnership with Compagnie Française des Pétroles, using the first mobile drilling barge to be built in Europe, also proved a swift success. Sheikh Shakbut officially started the first oil flowing from Abu Dhabi Marine Areas' Umm Shaif field, 60 miles offshore from the Gulf state's mainland, late in October 1962.

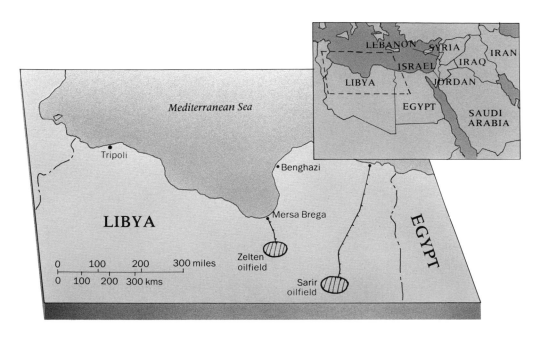

LEBANON SYRIA
ISRAEL IRAN
LIBYA IRAQ
JORDAN
EGYPT
SAUDI ARABIA

Mediterranean Sea

Tripoli

•Benghazi

Mersa Brega

LIBYA

0   100   200   300 miles
0   100   200   300 kms

Zelten oilfield

Sarir oilfield

EGYPT

After early disappointments, BP's exploration effort in Libya bore fruit in the early 1960s when, in partnership with Bunker Hunt, it discovered the Sarir field.

83

By then BP was even more excited about its find in Libya. The company had acquired its first concessions in the largely desert country west of Egypt in 1957. It was one of 18 companies granted a multitude of small exploration areas by the Libyan oil minister, who was determined to prevent his country falling into the hands of a single company.

BP's early surveys were disappointing and it was close to pulling out when, in April 1959, Standard Oil (New Jersey) made a big discovery at Zelten, about 200 miles inland from Benghazi. Libya's oil proved to be very low in sulphur and easily refined into light, 'clean' products such as petrol. BP rapidly changed its mind about quitting and, in partnership with Bunker Hunt Oil, one of the independents, found a ten-billion-barrel field at Sarir, about 150 miles south-east of Zelten. It was one of nine discovered in the 18-month scramble that followed Standard Oil (New Jersey)'s strike. In 1967, a BP tanker loaded the first cargo from the partners' new terminal at Tobruk, connected to the oilfield by a 300-mile pipeline. A year later, Libya's oil production exceeded that of Kuwait and almost matched Iran's.

These new discoveries gave BP vast crude oil reserves with seemingly limitless production potential. The company's output rose from 740,000 barrels a day in 1954 to 1,500,000 in 1960 and 3,800,000 barrels in 1970. Outside the USA, only Standard Oil (New Jersey) was a larger oil producer in the non-communist world than BP by the mid-1960s.

While oil gushed from BP's wells in ever-increasing volumes, the market for oil was also growing fast. The world economy prospered and the new 'consumer society' was fuelled more and more by oil in preference to other forms of energy. Buoyant demand helped BP's marketers achieve big increases in sales. In 1954 the European and West African marketing interests of the Atlantic Refining Company of Philadelphia were acquired. In the UK, Shell-Mex and BP acquired the National Benzole Company in 1957. Sales grew rapidly, but not as fast as in continental Europe, which

BP refinery at Aden, 1950s.

BP service station in Dakar, Senegal, West Africa, 1956.

A scientist at BP's Sunbury research centre distills motor fuel samples, 1958.

Over the years, BP films have won many prizes, none more prestigious than the Oscar awarded in 1961 for the short documentary, *Giuseppina*.

became the mainstay of BP's downstream business. In 1958 two small refining and marketing organizations in Italy were purchased. In 1965 BP added Finland to its marketing territory.

By 1970 continental Europe accounted for nearly half of BP's sales of refined oil products, compared with little more than a quarter in 1954. At the same time, BP's European refining capacity grew apace. By 1970 more than two-thirds of BP's refining was carried out in the UK and in mainland Europe. The company had come a long way since 1950, when the Abadan refinery accounted for three-quarters of BP's refining throughput.

Along with the increase in the volume of refined products came improved quality. In lubricants, BP's 'Energol' brand was superseded by multigrade oil sold as 'Visco-Static', later replaced by 'Super Visco-Static' and 'Visco 2000'. In the UK, retail petrol rationing had ended in 1950, but the reintroduction of branded and premium-grade petrols was not authorized until 1953. Once brands were allowed back on the forecourts, the launch of 'BP Super' was well received by the public. It was followed by a new, more advanced petrol, 'BP Super Plus', in the summer of 1956. The next year, every Formula 1 Grand Prix race counting for the World Championship was won on BP products. The year after that, the BP logo and shield were updated to a new design that was to be used for 30 years.

Outside Europe, BP's business in marine bunkering and aviation fuels grew rapidly, and in Australia and New Zealand BP became sole owner of its downstream subsidiaries, purchasing the shareholdings held by their respective national governments.

In the Western hemisphere, BP began to market its products in Trinidad, where it had a small upstream interest, and in 1957 started selling in Canada. But the real prize was the US market. In 1958 BP reached agreement with Sinclair Oil Corporation for the formation of two joint companies. One was to sell BP's Middle East crude in the USA through Sinclair's downstream facilities. The other was to engage in exploration, primarily in Latin America. US controls on imports of Middle East crude, however, frustrated the downstream agreement with Sinclair.

In the East, BP entered Malaysia in 1964 by buying Maruzen Toyo, which owned and operated a refinery in Singapore. BP Malaysia was set up as a marketing company, followed by BP Singapore, formed after the governments of Malaysia and Singapore decided to separate. By the autumn of 1965 the first BP service stations were opened in Singapore.

Without retail marketing operations in two of the world's largest markets – the USA and Japan – BP's downstream business could not absorb its upstream production. The company was forced to resort to ever-larger bulk sales of crude oil to other oil companies. But there were other uses to which the company's great oil supplies could be put, such as petrochemicals. The first step had been taken in 1947, when British Petroleum Chemicals was formed in partnership with the Distillers Company to make ethyl and isopropyl alcohols at Grangemouth. By 1960 the chemical company was manufacturing a whole range of petrochemicals and had opened its first polyethylene plant at Grangemouth. BP's French subsidiary had a large shareholding in Naphtachimie, which also was manufacturing polyethylene near the Lavéra refinery. In Germany BP formed a joint company with Bayer to manufacture petrochemicals. In 1965, BP bought the plastics interests of Mobil and early in 1967 paid £86m. for all Distillers' chemicals and plastics businesses, making BP the second largest chemicals group in the UK after ICI.

Meanwhile, research by BP France had discovered the possibilities of converting oil into proteins to help feed the growing population of the world. By 1968 BP was ready to construct a 4,000-tons-a-year plant at Grangemouth and a larger plant at Lavéra to make proteins to replace fishmeal in animal feed. With Kuwaiti crude at $1.50 a barrel, the economics looked good. In 1970 a new business, BP Proteins, was set up to take the process into commercial production.

BP's growing use of computers also led to the purchase of a computer programming company, later renamed Scicon.

As a result of all this expansion, the grandiose 'palace' on Finsbury Circus that Lutyens had designed for Anglo-Persian in the early 1920s was soon overcrowded. About 500 of the head office staff were moved out to Harlow in Essex. Others were accommodated in a new skyscraper 100 yards from Britannic House on the other side of Moorgate.

One thing that was not increasing, however, was the price of oil. From the mid-1950s to the end of the 1960s it had remained stable. This meant, after allowing for general price inflation, that it was really falling. The oil-producing states blamed the oil companies. Maurice Bridgeman, who succeeded Gass as chairman in 1960, took the criticisms to heart. 'It is unfortunate,' he said plaintively, 'that those who try to play their part in the progressive development of natural resources on the basis of freely negotiated agreements . . . should in some quarters be branded as exploiters and imperialists.' He tried hard to demonstrate that this charge was untrue. 'To say that an integrated oil company makes a profit at the producing stage is like saying that the profit of the village baker is derived from mixing his dough,' Bridgeman argued in his annual statement in 1962. 'The baker cannot make his profit until he has bought an oven, and probably a van as well, and has baked and delivered his bread and been paid for it.'

In other words, the oil industry required massive capital investment which, at a time of low oil prices and rising taxes, was not as remunerative as it had generally been in the past. Most of Bridgeman's annual statements indicated that for one reason or another the previous year had been unusually difficult. But in spite of everything the group grew steadily and at the beginning of 1967 BP's directors were confidently forecasting a net profit for the year of more than £100m.

During the 1960s, new materials revolutionized the design of homes and offices. This living-room of a 1969 show-house is largely made from and furnished by materials derived from BP Chemicals' products.

Sir Maurice Bridgeman, who joined the company in 1926, was chairman from 1960 to 1969. He served as Anglo-Persian's representative in New York in the 1930s, experience that later proved useful in paving the way for BP's wider presence in the country after 1970.

Chapter Eleven

OPEC and the Oil Weapon

Left The *British Captain* in Table Bay, off Cape Town, South Africa, in 1972. With the Suez Canal closed after the Six Day Arab-Israeli war, the only way BP could bring Iranian oil to Europe was round the Cape of Good Hope.

The first warning that 1967 was going to be a tough year came in January, when Syria once again cut the pipeline from Iraq to the Mediterranean, this time for two months. This was just a foretaste of what was to come.

The Israeli air force launched its pre-emptive strike against its Arab neighbours' ominous preparations to 'liquidate' the Jewish state on the morning of Monday 5 June 1967. Six days later the west bank of the Jordan River and the Golan Heights were under the control of Israel's armed forces and the whole length of the Suez canal was in their sights. Defeated in the field, the Arab states brought their oil weapon into play. Saudi Arabia, Kuwait, Iraq, Libya and Algeria banned shipments to the USA, Britain and West Germany as friends of Israel and the canal was closed indefinitely by scuttled ships. Although the Shah did not join the embargo, the only way BP could bring Iranian oil to Europe was round the Cape of Good Hope.

The first Suez crisis in 1956 had sparked a revolution in oil transport. Within a decade the size of tankers had mushroomed from less than 50,000 tons to 200,000 tons and more. But the Arab action still reduced Middle Eastern supplies to Europe by six million barrels a day and the situation worsened late in June when civil war broke out in Nigeria. The result was a frantic rush for tankers.

Right Smoke billows from ruptured oil tanks at an Egyptian refinery after an artillery duel across the Suez Canal between Israeli and Arab forces in late October 1967.

BP's assistant general manager in charge of oil supply, a rising young economist named Peter Walters, was mowing the lawn at his London home one Saturday when George Mackenzie, head of ship chartering, telephoned him. 'We've just had Aristotle Onassis on the phone,' Mackenzie said. 'He wants to know whether we want to charter his tankers.'

Right The *British Duchess* carries a cargo of Iranian crude through the Suez Canal before its closure.

A deal with Greek shipping millionaire, Aristotle Onassis, owner of the world's biggest independent fleet, ensured BP's Middle East oil continued to reach Europe and the USA, despite the blocking of the Suez canal.

Production unit and hydrogen sulphide columns, Iran, 1969.

'What, all of them?' Walters asked. The Greek shipping millionaire owned two-and-a-half million tons of tankers, the biggest independent fleet in the world. 'Yes,' came the reply. 'It's an all-or-nothing deal for one year. He is giving us a first option until noon today.'

Onassis's asking price was high, but although BP's own fleet totalled four million tons, with a similar tonnage under long-term charter, its capacity was still not large enough to meet the immediate demand. Walters called back at ten minutes to 12 and told his colleague to accept. 'Sunday was a difficult day,' he said afterwards, but by Monday charter rates were already increasing and a week later they had doubled. Walters had made the right decision.

The Arab embargo was a sign of the growing assertiveness of the main oil-exporting states. In 1959 the oil companies had cut their 'posted' prices for Persian Gulf and Venezuelan crude oils, following an unexpected flood of Soviet oil into Western markets. In response, Iran, Saudi Arabia, Kuwait, Iraq and Venezuela had founded the Organisation of Petroleum Exporting Countries in 1960 to co-ordinate the petroleum policies of oil-exporting countries.

OPEC's initial impact was small. For a long time the oil companies, including BP, ignored it. The Cold War deprived the oil states of political clout and Saudi Arabia was opposed to cutting its production, which undermined the only practical weapon at their disposal. At best, OPEC succeeded in stabilizing posted prices at around $1.65 a barrel throughout the 1960s. Although world consumption of oil doubled during the decade, output more than kept pace, with the enormous new discoveries in North Africa, such as BP's in Libya, adding to huge increases by the Middle Eastern producers.

In practice, the effect of the Arab embargo was short-lived. The US relaxed controls on domestic production. Iran and Venezuela raised their output and the international oil companies redistributed supplies. Within

a month it was apparent that more than enough oil was available to meet demand. The Arab 'oil weapon' had backfired, and the countries which had launched it were the principal losers. At the end of August, the Arab states lifted their embargo on exports. But it had hurt the oil companies as well. BP was the worst hit by additional freight and other costs totalling £85m., although higher oil prices clawed back £50m.

Further shocks were to come. BP's general manager in Libya, Roger Bexon, was sitting in his office in Benghazi on 1 September 1969 when the door opened and an army officer without insignia demanded the use of the company's radio. It soon became obvious that there was no real resistance to what was equally clearly a military coup led by a young lieutenant-colonel named Muammar al-Ghaddafi.

Bexon soon found himself involved in negotiations with Ghaddafi over oil prices and taxes, both of which were raised. Libya's new ruler had an unnerving habit of placing his revolver on the table at the start of their meetings. In 1971 the revolutionary leader presented the companies operating in his country with a set of 'non-negotiable' demands which added

Laying a pipeline in Kuwait in 1967, at that time the source of almost one-quarter of the Middle East's oil production.

BP chairman Sir Maurice Bridgeman (right) visits the Zakum oilfield, offshore Abu Dhabi, in March 1968.

90 cents a barrel to the price they were paying Libya for their oil. Ghaddafi's new terms leapfrogged a deal giving the Gulf states 35 cents a barrel more, which had been agreed only a short time earlier in Tehran. Worse was to come for the oil companies.

Towards the end of 1971 the UK withdrew its forces from the Persian Gulf, which had been under British protection for more than a century. The

Right Colonel Ghaddafi, who seized power in Libya in a military coup in 1969, overturned existing oil-producing agreements with foreign operators. Two years later he nationalized BP's interests in the country.

move was part of an overall withdrawal from east of Suez. Iran leaped into the power vacuum and seized some small Arab islands near the Strait of Hormuz. Ghaddafi promptly nationalized BP's share of its joint venture with Bunker Hunt in protest at the British failure to prevent this act of 'aggression' against the Arabs. By the end of 1972 Iraq had nationalized the Iraq Petroleum Company, and Saudi Arabia, Abu Dhabi and Qatar had forced the oil companies to agree to 25-per-cent government participation in their concessions, rising to 51 per cent in ten years.

Not to be outdone, the Shah summoned BP and the other members of Iranian Oil Participants to St Moritz, Switzerland, in January 1973. He presented them with the choice of losing all their rights in seven years' time, or accepting a new contract that would hand control of the oilfields over to the state immediately, in return for their becoming 'good customers' entitled to buy his country's oil for the next 20 years. With regret, the oil companies accepted the second option. On 16 March the Shah announced proudly that the oil companies had 'totally surrendered' and declared the St Moritz agreement a 'historic document' which finally implemented the Nationalization Act of 1951 'in its fullest sense'.

Any satisfaction the oil states might have felt with their gains was undermined by the gathering pace of inflation in the industrialized world. The six Gulf oil producers summoned the oil companies to talks in Vienna, beginning on 8 October 1973. BP's team, led by Peter Walters, included Roger Bexon, who was to sit on a sub-committee charged with agreeing a premium for low-sulphur oil. Two days before the discussions opened, Nasser's successor, Anwar al-Sadat, desperate to break the six-year stale-

Egyptian president Anwar al-Sadat's surprise attack on Israel in October 1973 began the Yom Kippur War, which precipitated a worldwide oil shock.

mate which was keeping Egypt bankrupt and powerless, launched a surprise attack on Israel's forces in the Sinai. The Yom Kippur War had begun.

The first bargaining session between the delegation representing the
British and American companies and the six Gulf oil ministers, led by
Sheikh Ahmed Zaki Yamani of Saudi Arabia, ended in less than an hour.
The BP delegate returned to his hotel with a long face. 'What happened?'
Bexon asked. 'They want another three dollars,' Walters answered grimly.
The companies had been prepared to cede 45 cents, an offer which the size
of OPEC's demand made seem paltry.

In any case, all the main protagonists were waiting on the outcome of
the conflict in the Middle East. No one in Vienna wanted to break off negotiations until the picture cleared. Bexon found himself engaged in an
extended debate with a trio led by the oil minister of Abu Dhabi about the
sulphur premium, in order to keep up the pretence that the conference was
continuing. Half the time the Western oilmen watched television for news
about the war. To begin with, Egypt did well and the Arab oil negotiators
were cheerful and constructive. But, as Israel rallied, the atmosphere
became gloomier and the bargaining less promising.

The sulphur sideshow ended after three days when the principal negotiations resumed, only to fail equally swiftly. Four days later the six Gulf
producers unilaterally increased the posted price of their crude oil from $3
to $5 a barrel and raised their take from $1.75 to $3. The Arab states also
announced that they would cut production by a cumulative 5 per cent
monthly until Israel withdrew from the territories it had captured in the
Six Day War. Two months later they raised their share to $7 a barrel,

After a slow start, OPEC's
power increased dramatically
during the 1970s. Because of
his country's huge oil reserves,
Saudi Arabia's oil minister,
Sheikh Yamani (centre), played
a pivotal role during this
period.

Sir Eric Drake (right) and George King, then general manager and later managing director of BP Tankers, check out new routes for oil tankers through the English Channel in 1972. Drake was chairman from 1969 to 1975, a period of turmoil in world oil markets.

pushing the posted price to $11.75. Throughout the world, governments panicked as consumers queued for petrol at the pumps, industry ground to a halt for lack of fuel and prices paid for individual cargoes of oil escalated to unheard-of heights.

In Britain, the energy crisis was particularly acute, owing to the Conservative government's confrontation with the coalminers. Edward Heath summoned Sir Eric Drake, who four years earlier had succeeded Sir Maurice Bridgeman as chairman of BP, and Sir Frank McFadzean of Shell to a meeting. The Prime Minister requested them not to reduce oil supplies to the UK. Both refused, McFadzean on the grounds that his group was 60 per cent Dutch-owned. Drake, with the British government still a majority shareholder in BP, was not so well placed, but resisted equally strongly. 'Are you asking me to do this as a shareholder or as a government?' he said. 'If you are asking me as a shareholder, you should realize that all our European subsidiaries could be nationalized in retaliation. If you are asking me as a government, give me a piece of paper to say that is what you want me to do, so I can plead *force majeure*.' 'You know very well I can't do that,' the architect of Britain's entry into the Common Market replied angrily.

The power shortages that winter closed Britain's factories for two days a week in January 1974 and led to victory for the coalminers and the fall of the Conservative government. That year, however, the Arab states dropped their embargo and oil supplies began to rise once more.

But the oil-producing countries continued to assert their control over supplies. The Nigerian government had already taken a 35-per-cent participation in BP's oil concession in 1973. In 1974 this was raised to 55 per cent. The same year, Kuwait took a 60-per-cent stake in its oil industry, and Abu Dhabi and Qatar, which had already taken 25 per cent, raised their participation to the same level. In 1975 Kuwait nationalized the remaining interests of the oil companies. Shortly afterwards, so did Qatar.

BP's world had turned upside down again. Its entire integrated business was built on access to the huge reserves of low-cost equity crude oil which it had discovered, mainly in the Middle East. In 1971 the company lifted more than four million barrels a day of equity crude, of which more than 80 per cent came from the Middle East and most of the rest from Africa. Purchases of crude made up only 10 per cent of its total liftings. By 1976 the position was reversed. BP's production of equity crude was down to 460,000 barrels a day, little more than 10 per cent of the quantity five years earlier. Meanwhile purchases of crude had risen dramatically, to reach nearly three million barrels a day, or more than 80 per cent of its total supplies.

The effects of the oil shock were much more widely felt. The quadrupling of prices by OPEC brought huge changes to every corner of the world economy. Wealth was transferred from the industrialized nations to the oil exporters on a scale that was hard to grasp. The combined oil revenues of the oil exporters rose from $23 billion in 1972 to $140 billion in 1977. The economies of oil-consuming nations suffered profoundly. The

The 215,000-ton *British Pioneer* in 1971. A decade previously, the average size of tankers had been less than 50,000 deadweight tons.

Paris No. 7 wellsite in Iran, 1969.

USA's gross national product fell by 6 per cent between 1973 and 1975. In Japan, the continuous economic growth achieved since the end of World War II was brought to a halt. Europe, where BP's downstream business was concentrated, was also plunged into recession.

BP seemed to be defying gravity when it announced that profits in 1974 were well up on the previous year. It was a deceptive result; the increase was due to a one-off jump in the value of BP's oil stocks after the price hike of 1973. In March 1975 Drake warned shareholders that the immediate outlook was not altogether reassuring. However, against the loss of BP's traditional sources of crude in the Middle East, he was able to point to exciting developments in new oil provinces where BP had major interests: the North Sea and Alaska.

Chapter Twelve

The North Sea

Left Forties Bravo, one of the four steel platforms built to tap the prolific Forties field. The field, the first major oil strike in the UK sector of the North Sea, began production in 1975.

The first oil from the North Sea officially arrived in the UK on Monday 3 November 1975. That was when Queen Elizabeth II pressed a button on the computer controlling the western end of the new pipeline stretching 110 miles from BP's Forties field to Cruden Bay, near Peterhead in Scotland. With daily production expected to be 500,000 barrels a day by the end of 1977, the four-billion-barrel Forties discovery would supply 20 per cent of the UK's oil requirements. Including its interest in the newly discovered fields east of the Shetland islands, BP's North Sea oil finds might not replace its lost holdings in the Middle East, but they would make a very welcome contribution.

BP had been looking for oil in the UK since the end of World War I. Small finds had been made in the English counties of Derbyshire, Hampshire, Lancashire, Nottinghamshire and Yorkshire, and in Scotland, but by 1959 British oil production was only 500,000 barrels a year. A search for natural gas on behalf of British Gas had proved equally disappointing. But the discovery of what was estimated to be the world's second largest gasfield at Groningen in the Netherlands in August 1959 by Shell-Esso had changed everything. Suddenly the prospects of finding gas under the North Sea in the region off the Dutch coast were exciting.

Right Helicopters are the workhorses of the North Sea, transferring workers to the offshore platforms. Bright orange survival suits are worn for even the shortest journeys as a basic safety precaution.

Coincidentally, the British government's interest in offshore exploration was sparked by agreement in the United Nations to extend sovereign rights over territorial waters so that coastal states would have mineral rights to the continental shelf out to a water depth of 200 metres. Although the new international law did not come into force until 1964, by then BP and Shell had carried out a joint seismic survey of the sea-bed east of Great Yarmouth, the closest area to the Groningen field.

BP started drilling in June 1965. It chose an area off East Anglia named

Flaring BP's first gas from the
North Sea aboard the *Sea Gem*,
7 December 1965.

Drilling bits, 1979.

Workers on North Sea
platforms typically spend two
weeks offshore followed by two
weeks' home leave. Good
facilities for leisure and a high
standard of catering help to
make off-duty periods relaxing
and enjoyable.

West Sole, using a 13-year-old American drilling barge, *Sea Gem*, which
had been converted in France for the harsh conditions in the North Sea.
At the beginning of October BP announced that it had found gas at 10,000
ft and early in December a test of the well indicated a production rate of
ten million cubic feet of gas a day, enough to power a city as big as
Coventry. The triumph was followed by tragedy. On Boxing Day 1965 *Sea
Gem* lurched to one side while the legs on which it sat on the sea-bed were
being jacked up. An hour-and-a-half later it turned turtle and sank.
Thirteen of the 32 men on board lost their lives. The official inquiry into
the disaster identified several likely and possibly cumulative causes for the
collapse but no blame was apportioned. The underlying message, however,
was already clear to the oil industry. The North Sea was a dangerous place
and future drilling platforms would have to be much stronger if they were
to be safe.

BP signed a contract to supply the national gas grid from its West Sole
field at an incentive price roughly 50 per cent higher than was paid for subsequent supplies from other finds. It earned the bonus. Laying the 45-mile
pipeline to the company's new terminal at Easington, just north of the
Humber estuary, proved to be a tough and expensive struggle against
storms, a boulder-strewn sea-bottom and even the occasional wartime
mine. But the first natural gas reached Easington on 6 March 1967, less
than 18 months after the first hole was drilled.

In spite of the gas finds, few people thought the North Sea a good
prospect for oil. It took the discovery in 1969 by Phillips Petroleum of the
Ekofisk field, 175 miles south-west of Stavanger in the Norwegian sector
of the North Sea, to stimulate the search. Even Phillips had been on the
verge of abandoning its efforts.

BP was particularly sceptical. It had been looking for oil in the UK for
nearly 50 years but had never found a major field. Even after Ekofisk, BP's

exploration efforts were far from full-blooded. 'There won't be a major field there,' Drake told Reuters in April 1970, although adding that BP had an obligation to go on looking. Six months later the company announced the discovery of the Forties field, the first major oil strike in the British sector.

BP's ability to find oil was becoming legendary. The company's exploration team was far from large, perhaps 200 geologists and geophysicists in 1970, a tenth of the number employed by groups such as Esso and Shell. But its success ratio was extraordinary. One reason, undoubtedly, was the company's experience of major oil deposits. For nearly 70 years its geologists and engineers had been poring over several of the world's largest oilfields. They had built up an intimate understanding of these vast and complicated geological structures that permeated BP's entire exploration approach. From George Reynolds onwards, BP's field men seemed almost to have a nose for oil.

The discovery of the Forties field was an example. BP's robust new drilling platform, the 15,000-ton *Sea Quest*, was under an obligation to drill a well for Hamilton Oil on an undersea structure which had been named McNutt's Half Dome. Harry Warman, BP's assistant exploration manager, was not impressed by the results of the seismic survey that revealed it – and in any case he thought the name silly. So he altered *Sea Quest's* drilling programme and sent the platform to a location on the company's own concession. Warman insisted later that it was not luck: 'It had been picked as a drillable structure and it would have been drilled. I merely changed the sequence. That helped to find it maybe a year earlier.' But he admitted that BP had no idea that the sandstone into which *Sea Quest* drilled contained oil in commercial quantities.

BP announced its find at 8.30 p.m. on 19 October 1970, waiting until the New York Stock Exchange had closed. That did not stop the markets from going wild with excitement or the national newspapers from trumpeting the strike the next day. It was a year before the company disclosed that two more wells had confirmed Forties as a world-class field, capable of producing at least 400,000 barrels a day. By then, other discoveries had proved that the North Sea had a production potential of at least two million barrels a day, of which half would come from the British sector.

The next challenge was to bring the new discoveries into production. Forties, for example, lay under more than 350 ft of water. Bringing the oil ashore would require the largest deep-water submarine pipeline ever laid. BP set up a computer study to analyse the stresses involved in laying a line in 400 ft of water, as well as how to protect it when it was in place by burying it in a trench gouged in the sea-floor. The production pipeline would be safe from the conditions on the surface, but would have to survive the harsh tides, the corrosive effect of salt water and the rugged state of the bottom. The lessons learned in laying the pipeline from West Sole were valuable but little was known about the real conditions 100 miles off the Scottish coast. The existing Admiralty charts were based on surveys made in Victorian times. A full-scale oceanographic survey was required, much

A historic moment is captured as BP's first tot of North Sea oil is poured, in 1970, on board *Sea Quest*.

Engineer on BP's Magnus field, the UK's most northerly oilfield. Magnus, discovered in 1974 in 186 metres of water in the East Shetland basin, started production in 1982.

A standby vessel supports a production platform in BP's Forties field, 1976.

Margaret Thatcher, MP, then leader of the Opposition and later British Prime Minister, visits BP's drilling platform, *Sea Quest*, on 9 September 1975.

of which was carried out by BP's marine sciences group, part of the research organization at Sunbury.

The biggest task, however, was manufacturing the production platforms. BP chose to order two at once. Both were tall enough to stand 140 ft above the surface of the sea, which meant a total height of 560 ft. The base of each of the four gigantic legs stood 200 ft apart and was pinned to the sea-bed by piles reaching down another 300 ft. With the tragic fate of the *Sea Gem* still fresh in mind, BP was determined its Forties platforms would stand rock steady for at least 40 years, firm enough to weather a once-a-century storm bringing winds of over 130 miles per hour and monster waves more than 90 ft high.

A major problem was to provide enough storage capacity to enable the platforms to drill all the year round. As winter conditions were likely to restrict unloading from supply vessels to as little as once a month, each platform stocked enough material to drill a complete well – 17,000 ft of well casing, 500 tons of mud and 600 tons of cement. Altogether each platform required over 50,000 tons of steel, more than had been used to make the Forth railway bridge in Scotland.

The platforms were just the beginning. At the other end of the 100-mile pipeline the new Cruden Bay terminal was itself only a staging-post, sending some of the Forties oil on to BP's Grangemouth refinery and the rest to a special shipping terminal in the Firth of Forth, a mile below the famous bridges and capable of receiving the 200,000-ton tankers that were becoming the industry standard. Another pipeline connected the terminal to an inland storage tank which was carefully landscaped to preserve the natural beauty of the firth.

By any standards development of the Forties field was a tremendous undertaking. Other, even more testing, discoveries were beginning to be exploited further north, but Forties was the first. Its development stretched BP's technical skills to an extraordinary extent, not to mention its finances. The company's initial estimate of the cost of Forties was £175m., but by the time the Queen pressed the symbolic button at Dyce this had risen to £400m. By 1979 BP had invested more than £1 billion in North Sea oil. This included its share of spending on Europe's largest crude-oil terminal, Sullom Voe in the Shetlands, where the first supplies had just arrived from the Brent field, owned by Shell, and the Ninian field, in which BP owned 13 per cent. BP had a controlling interest in the smaller Buchan field, which was about to go into production. The company had also decided to develop its latest discovery, Magnus, on the inhospitable northern rim of the East Shetlands basin, at a cost of another £1,300m.

Finding the capital was a continual task. Fortunately BP was still making a great deal of money from Middle Eastern oil, even though its direct holdings were so diminished. It had sold 45 per cent of its shareholding in Abu Dhabi Marine Areas to Japanese companies for more than $700m. in 1972. But Lord Greenhill, who had been appointed one of the government's two BP directors in 1974 after retiring as Permanent Secretary at the Foreign Office, found the huge sums the company seemed to be constantly raising distinctly alarming. He was also uncomfortably aware that the government he represented was contributing nothing.

Greenhill and the other government director, the ex-postal union leader Tom Jackson, found their position complicated by the insistence of the Labour Secretary of State for Energy, Tony Benn, that BP's relationship with the government should be through his department and not through the Treasury and the Foreign Office as in the past. Benn was convinced that the development of North Sea oil and gas should be run by the state, if only to avoid its falling under the control of international oil companies. His first instinct was simply to nationalize BP. After all, the government already held a controlling interest, didn't it?

Indeed, the government and the Bank of England together held just over two-thirds of BP's shares. In the late 1960s Burmah Oil had embarked on an ambitious programme of acquisitions, investment in tankers and exploration in the North Sea and elsewhere. It had borrowed heavily and used its 23-per-cent shareholding in BP as collateral for the loans. In 1974 share prices collapsed following the energy crisis and the defeat of Edward Heath's government. Burmah Oil was rescued from bankruptcy by the Bank of England, which in return took the BP shares, valuing them at the ultra-low price at which they were quoted on the London Stock Exchange.

Benn soon found, however, that BP was not willing to be nationalized. He recorded in his diary that Eric Drake went to see him on 15 July 1975: 'He said that Government holding of British Petroleum shares must be kept below 50 per cent because it would destroy the credibility of the company in the United States, in New Zealand, and elsewhere – BP operates in 80 countries. Therefore, he wanted the BP Burmah shares sold off in the open market but not to foreign governments.'

99

Tony Benn's first task as Energy Secretary in the Labour government was to turn the valve that symbolically started the flow of the first North Sea oil. Accompanying him on 18 June 1975 at BP's Kent refinery on the Isle of Grain was Fred Hamilton (left), head of Hamilton Oil, the small US independent oil company that developed the UK's first offshore producing field.

Her Majesty Queen Elizabeth II, accompanied by BP chairman, Sir Eric Drake, presses the button to start the flow of oil from the Forties field to Grangemouth refinery on 3 November 1975.

The company reminded the government that its shareholding did not entitle it to interfere in BP's day-to-day commercial activities, pressing the point home by disinterring the original letter, written in 1914 by Sir John Bradbury of the Treasury, limiting the use of the government veto to fundamental strategic questions, such as those touching on foreign policy.

The Secretary of State for Energy did not give in easily. David Steel, who succeeded Drake as chairman at the end of 1975, lost count of the number of times he used to call on Benn at the end of the day. 'I could always tell when he was going to twist my arm because he'd say: "Oh David, have a whisky," and he'd get a little bottle out of a cupboard somewhere.'

Benn met with further frustrations. He discovered that Britain's membership of the European Community prevented the government from reserving North Sea oil licences for UK nationals. It also limited the British National Oil Corporation, the state-owned company Benn had set up, to a half-share in all new concessions granted in the British sector. Most other members of the Labour cabinet were at best lukewarm to the idea of nationalizing the oil industry. Denis Healey, Chancellor of the Exchequer, was the most powerful voice against it.

Above Even after 20 years' development, the North Sea is still yielding new fields. The Bruce field, commissioned in 1993, is now BP's biggest gas producer in the North Sea.

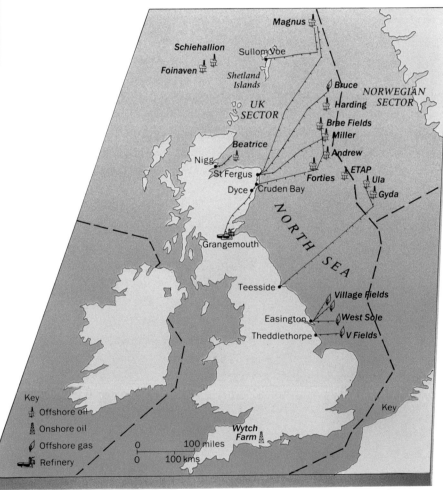

Map showing BP's principal upstream interests in the UK and Norwegian waters in 1995.

Left BP's activities in the North Sea also extended into Norwegian waters. Installation of the production jacket for the Ula platform, June 1985.

101

In his letter of 20 May 1914 Sir John Bradbury, Joint Permanent Secretary of the Treasury, promised no government interference in Anglo-Persian's commercial operations. The letter was used to defend the company against intervention by the Labour government in the mid-1970s.

however, contemplate that both the *ex officio* Directors should always be present at Committee meetings. Occasions may arise when it may be desirable that both the *ex officio* Directors should be present, but as a general rule the presence of only one of them would be necessary. Indeed, at some meetings it may not be necessary that either of them should be present.

3. You are at liberty to make such use of this letter as you may think fit at the proposed meetings of the shareholders.

I am,
Gentlemen,
Your obedient Servant,

Jn. Bradbury

Messrs. The Anglo-Persian Oil Company (Limited).
Winchester House,
Old Broad Street,
London, E.C.

[563]   PRINTED AT THE FOREIGN OFFICE BY C. R. HARRISON.—19/5/1914.

The economy was in grave difficulties. Far from taking over BP, the Treasury was keen to sell part of its holding, beginning with the Burmah stake, as soon as it could get a decent price.

Benn's lingering hopes of nationalization were finally dashed at the end of 1976, when the UK's financial plight drove the new Prime Minister, James Callaghan, to seek a loan from the International Monetary Fund. In June 1977 the government put 66 million of its BP shares up for sale at a price of 845p a share (equivalent to 70p a share today, after adjusting for share splits and capitalization issues). The 'sale of the century', handled by a consortium of nine merchant banks, headed by S G Warburg, raised £564m. for the hard-pressed Treasury.

The price reflected the recovery in the stock-market valuation of BP, much of it due to a growing appreciation of the worth of its North Sea oil and gas reserves. In spite of finds by other groups, more than half the crude oil extracted from the British sector of the North Sea so far had come from BP's discoveries. They were not the company's only successes. A third of the way round the world, an even more exciting development was coming to fruition.

Above Drilling floor on board a production platform in BP's Clyde oilfield, January 1992.

Chapter Thirteen

North to Alaska

Left A Prudhoe Bay worker faces the bitter Arctic cold that can cause frostbite to unprotected skin in a matter of seconds.

Alaska was first mentioned within BP in a world survey of oil prospects compiled by the company's exploration department in 1952, shortly after the expulsion from Iran. The north of Alaska was included because of oil and gas discoveries made there by the US Geological Service, which had spent the years after World War II looking for new strategic fuel reserves for the American Navy. Admittedly, the finds were not large. On the other hand, the 100,000-sq.-mile plain of frozen tundra sloping down from the Brooks Range to the Arctic Ocean clearly contained several big geological structures of the kind that the company was familiar with in the Middle East. However, the North Slope was only one of many prospects around the world. The harsh conditions there, as well as a shortage of dollars, pushed exploration in the 49th state towards the bottom of the list.

In 1957, BP acquired some small oil wells in the Kern River area of California in the process of expanding its interests in Trinidad and Canada. By world standards, the wells were far from economic, but US support for

Right BP's first well at Prudhoe Bay on the North Slope of Alaska, spudded in on 20 November 1969, was named Put River No. 1, after the River Putuligayuk.

domestic oil prices meant they gave BP an income of $2m. to $3m. a year. This was worth twice as much if used for exploration as it could be set against tax at a rate of 50 cents to the dollar. Ironically, BP's more ambitious plans to import Middle Eastern oil into the USA in partnership with Sinclair ran up against the same protectionist measures. But BP's Californian income financed its share of a joint exploration programme with Sinclair, which was quickly rewarded with a small, but commercial, discovery in Colombia.

In the middle of 1957, a small company named Richfield Oil struck oil

Oil tanker in Prince William Sound, Alaska.

Oil production continues all year round at Prudhoe Bay.

near Anchorage in the south of Alaska, sparking off an exploration boom. Sinclair was keen to take part. However, Peter Cox, BP's chief geologist, had just returned from a flight across Alaska, during which he had remarked on the similarity between the foothills of the Brooks Range and the Zagros mountains in Iran. Soon afterwards, Cox was put in charge of BP's exploration and in February 1959 received a report from his men in the field which stated that the North Slope contained 'a wealth of drillable anticlines on the Iranian scale, with lengths of the order of 20 miles'.

As the attention of every other oil company focused on the search near Anchorage, BP found it easy to pick up leases near the US Navy's discoveries on the North Slope. By the beginning of April it had acquired leases over 50,000 acres and options over another 100,000. The first exploration team was soon in the field to take advantage of the Arctic summer, when the snow melted enough for the rocks to be seen. Even so the weather was often terrible, confining the geologists to their tents for days at a time.

By 1963 it was apparent that Cox had been wrong about the potential of the Brooks Range. BP's attention shifted further north to an area in which aerial photography and seismic surveys had located several large structures near Umiat, where the US Navy had found its oil. In the summer of 1963 a Canadian drilling rig was floated 2,000 miles down the Mackenzie River into the Arctic Ocean and then along the coast to the Colville River, which ran down to Alaska's north coast from Umiat. During the next 18 months, six wells were drilled, in temperatures so cold that steel fractured and normal lubricants froze solid. Oil and gas were eventually found, but only traces, not in commercial quantities.

BP, however, had continued its wider surveys while drilling was going on, led by a young Scottish geologist, Jim Spence. During the winter of 1963–4 his team located a huge underground dome of rock near the Colville River and a smaller faulted structure a little to the east, at Prudhoe Bay. Spence was fascinated by the second find, which tilted one way and then the other in a manner which suggested oil might have collected below it. In September 1964 BP asked Alaska to put the land up for competitive bidding. The state decided to offer the Colville area and, in the absence of any other real interest, BP acquired 318,000 acres at an average price of less than $6 an acre.

Nine months later the first land at Prudhoe Bay was put up for auction. By now other oil companies were beginning to take more interest in BP's lonely quest. Disheartened by the failures in the Brooks Range, Sinclair decided not to take part. Short of dollars, BP decided it could not compete with American companies for a lease in the centre. Instead, it gambled on the striking similarity of the Prudhoe Bay structure to its original field in Iran, where the oil-bearing rocks had proved to be thicker and more prolific around the edges. When the bidding closed, BP had acquired 90,000 acres around the rim at an average price of just over $16 an acre, compared with the $93 an acre the Richfield–Humble partnership paid for the central area.

Early in 1966 BP's well through the top of the Colville dome found

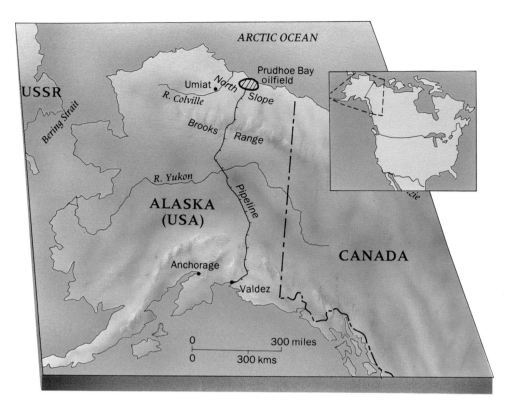

ARCTIC OCEAN

USSR

Umiat
R. Colville
North Slope
Prudhoe Bay oilfield

Bering Strait

Brooks Range

R. Yukon

ALASKA (USA)

Pipeline

Anchorage

Valdez

CANADA

Mackenzie

| 0 | | 300 miles |
| 0 | | 300 kms |

Map showing BP's early exploration interests in Alaska.

105

A production operator at the Endicott field in Alaska.

The historic signpost marking the Put River No. 1 well has corroded badly in the harsh weather conditions.

little oil. There might once have been a vast reservoir, but if so it had leaked away. In January 1967 more Prudhoe Bay leases were offered for sale. Once again BP went for land along the flanks, acquiring six blocks for about the same price per acre. It had paid approximately half the average spent by other oil companies, but BP was beginning to have a nasty feeling that even that was too much. Its second well at Colville was also dry, its eighth successive failure on the North Slope. BP had spent more than $30m. looking for oil in Alaska and, for all its high hopes, had found nothing. Early in 1968 the company decided enough was enough. It closed its Los Angeles office and packed its hired drilling rig ready for shipping back to Canada when the Colville River was free of ice.

Then in March Richfield Oil and Atlantic Refining, which had merged three years earlier to become Atlantic Richfield, struck oil in their last-chance well at the centre of the Prudhoe Bay structure. Three months later a second successful well seven miles away, drilled incidentally with the Canadian rig BP had relinquished, indicated a huge field. So, too, did an extravagant offer from Atlantic Richfield to buy all BP's Prudhoe Bay holdings. BP turned it down flat and barged a new rig through the Bering Strait. Drilling began in November and in March 1969 the Put River No. 1 well hit oil in large quantities.

The Prudhoe Bay field proved to be the largest ever found on the North American continent. Containing recoverable reserves estimated at 10 billion barrels of oil and 25 trillion cu. ft of gas, it was fully the equal of the giant fields in the Middle East and North Africa. And, as BP had hazarded,

The first BP gallons served in the USA filled the tank of an Oldsmobile in Atlanta, Georgia, on 29 April 1969.

Drilling under way in Alaska.

much of the oil was concentrated around the edge of the structure. When all the sums had been worked out, BP's leases were thought to contain 60 per cent of all the oil in Prudhoe Bay. Finding the oil was, of course, only the beginning. Bringing Prudhoe Bay into production and transporting the oil and gas 3,000 miles to eager consumers on the West Coast of the USA was a mammoth task that would demand vast expenditure. It was becoming obvious that BP needed to acquire direct access to the US market.

Its first chance came almost too soon. Towards the end of 1968 poor Sinclair Oil, which had passed over the chance to share BP's Prudhoe Bay blocks, had been forced to beg a merger with Atlantic Richfield to escape being taken over by Gulf & Western. US anti-trust legislation, however, had blocked the deal unless Sinclair's chain of 8,500 service stations and their back-up facilities in New England was sold off. Atlantic Richfield offered it to BP for $300m. – payable in instalments once production began at Prudhoe Bay. Eric Drake, about to become chairman in succession to Sir Maurice Bridgeman, took the chance and accepted. 'They were a rather anxious three months,' he said later. 'If our well at Put River had not been successful, it would have cost us $300m.'

He was soon gambling even more heavily on the Prudhoe Bay discovery. BP's directors decided the company needed more than the ex-Sinclair marketing outlets in the USA. Making the most of its Alaskan oil would require the financial and managerial resources of a large organization. Within days of the news of Put River No. 1's success, merger talks began with Standard Oil of Ohio. This still-powerful fragment of John D Rockefeller's dismembered empire was, like Sinclair, short of its own oil reserves. In the final agreement, BP swapped most of its Alaskan oil holdings, plus the ex-Sinclair marketing business it had bought from Atlantic Richfield, for an initial 25 per cent of Sohio's share capital. This holding was to rise to 54 per cent when Sohio's share of Prudhoe Bay production reached 600,000 barrels a day, forecast to be by January 1978. BP would continue to operate the Alaskan oilfield, but Sohio would manage the two companies' combined business in the rest of the USA.

The agreement was on the verge of completion when the US Justice Department blocked it on the grounds that it might contravene American anti-trust laws. To avoid protracted legal argument, Eric Drake flew to Washington and asked the Attorney-General in person what conditions he wanted to impose. Caught by surprise by this Alexandrian approach, the Justice Department gave its blessing, subject to relatively minor conditions, and the deal was completed on 1 January 1970.

BP, Atlantic Richfield and Humble Oil had already begun to develop their holdings as a single, unitized field, persuading the Alaskan state government to limit wells to one for each 640 acres covering the main field. Production was expected to begin at 500,000 barrels a day, plus another 500 million cu. ft of gas, and rise to over two million barrels a day by the end of the 1970s. All that remained was to spend one billion dollars on laying a pipeline the 800 miles from Prudhoe Bay to Valdez, a few miles east of Anchorage, where the oil and gas could be loaded at a new deep-water port into the supertankers which would then voyage down the Gulf of Alaska to California. BP took a 15-per-cent interest in the Trans-Alaska Pipeline System and Sohio another 33 per cent. In June 1969 TAPS confidently applied to the state of Alaska for a permit to lay the pipeline along the route it had chosen. Its application was refused.

Two groups were opposed to the pipeline. The Alaska Federation of Natives had been formed only in 1966, but the local tribes had been protesting at what they considered to be the illegal sale of their land to the USA by Russia for $7.2m. ever since the deal had been struck in 1867. The new federation was the first time all the tribal groups had come together. It had scored an immediate success by persuading the US Secretary of the Interior to halt grants of land under the terms of the 1958 Statehood Act. The land freeze, made official in January 1969, stopped the state leasing the oil companies a right of way for the pipeline until the question of native rights was settled. Sixty-six native Alaskans living on its proposed route also obtained an injunction in Washington against the pipeline being laid across their land without their consent.

Running in parallel with the issue of native rights was concern about the effect of oil development on Alaska's environment and wildlife. The fragility of the North Slope had been revealed at a very early stage. It took frighteningly little to destroy the thin mat of soil and vegetation that insulated the permafrost in the summer. An 18-inch drainage ditch could grow in as little as six weeks into a rushing torrent 6-ft deep and 10-ft wide, and the whole territory was scored by unhealed wounds made by tracked vehicles. Oil spills, too, had a disproportionate impact on the environment compared with their effect on the sands of the Middle East or even the waters of the North Sea, not to mention the usual litter of exploration and development, including thousands of abandoned fuel drums, each with its dregs.

BP was alert to the growing problem of oil pollution. It had set up a central anti-pollution advisory group in 1962. In the following year the company had helped organize an industry group to study methods of preventing air and water pollution in western Europe, where public concern had woken abruptly in 1967 when Amoco's *Torrey Canyon* ran aground off Land's End, spilling 117,000 tons of Kuwaiti crude into the English Channel. BP was also working with Atlantic Richfield on ways of minimizing the effect of the Prudhoe Bay oilfield on the tundra, such as diagonal drilling and gravel and styrofoam insulation. Contingency plans to contain oil spills had also been drawn up and the company flew empty fuel drums back to Anchorage, where they were sold for a small profit.

But the oil industry's concern for the environment was not enough to prevent its being taken by surprise when Friends of the Earth, the Environment Defense Fund and the Wilderness Society won a federal injunction against the right-of-way permit in April 1970.

The debate that followed over how to ensure that the pipeline did not pose a threat to the environment or to Alaska's wildlife was intense. The charge that pumping relatively warm oil through the pipe would melt the

From left to right, Dr (later Sir) Peter Kent, Harry Warman and Alwyne Thomas received the prestigious MacRobert Award for engineering and technology on 15 December 1970 in recognition of their geological and geophysical exploration work for BP in northern Alaska.

Since 1977, when the first oil from Prudhoe Bay travelled the 800 miles by pipeline to the Valdez marine terminal, many millions of barrels of Alaskan crude have been loaded on to tankers there.

The grandeur of the snowy mountains of the North Slope dwarfs the Trans-Alaska pipeline.

To avoid any risk that the relative warmth of the oil might melt the permafrost, the pipeline from Prudhoe Bay to Valdez is raised on pillars for about half its 800-mile length.

permafrost if it was buried underground led to agreement to raise the line on pillars for approximately half its length. But that posed questions about the effect of the elevated section on migrating herds of caribou. Would this bar them from their annual routes? Eric Drake commissioned the naturalist Peter Scott to make a report, and another was produced for the Trans-Alaska Pipeline System. Eventually it was decided to build ramps at major crossing points, but nobody knew what would happen. In the event, when the caribou did encounter the raised sections, they lowered their huge antlers and strolled nonchalantly underneath.

The first of the major hurdles was cleared in December 1971, when Congress approved the Native Claims Act, granting Alaska's indigenous population 40 million acres and $462m. in settlement of their hereditary claims. It was another two years before the environmental debate reached a point at which the Interior Secretary felt justified in issuing a federal permit for the pipeline. But finally, on 3 May 1974, the Alaska state right-of-way lease was signed.

The Trans-Alaska Pipeline System began transporting crude oil in mid-1977, five years later than planned. But by the end of 1978 it was operating at its full capacity of 1.2 million barrels a day, of which Sohio was entitled to more than half. BP's shareholding in Sohio rose accordingly to 54 per cent, only a few months later than originally planned. In 1979 the company's share of Sohio's profits was more than £500m.

It had taken a long time, but the company's commitment to new frontiers had finally paid off.

'In the last five years,' Sir David Steel, BP's chairman, told shareholders proudly, 'we in the British Petroleum group have added a million barrels a day to the oil supplies available to the world.'

Inuit children, native inhabitants of the region.

Oil companies such as BP that operate in Alaska pay careful attention to the conservation of this unique natural environment so that indigenous flora and fauna can flourish. In places, the Trans-Alaska pipeline is raised to allow migrating caribou to pass beneath it.

Chapter Fourteen

Diversification

In the 1970s, BP Nutrition companies were helping to launch the revolution in fish farming which transformed trout and salmon from luxuries to everyday fare in many markets. By the 1980s, BP Nutrition had become the world's number one supplier of aquaculture feed and know-how. In 1981, BP acquired T Skretting's salmon-feed business, a market leader in Norway.

BP was entitled to make the most of its successes in the North Sea and Alaska. They were no fluke, but rather the result of years of determined, expensive and long-term commitment to pioneering exploration and innovative development in two severe environments. The development of new sources of crude, however, was only a part of BP's response to the oil price shock and the loss of its huge Middle Eastern crude reserves. The take-over of the upstream sector by OPEC meant BP could no longer rely on cheap Middle Eastern and African crude as its main source of profits. The group's investments in transport, refining and marketing now had to stand on their own feet as profit-makers.

All oil companies felt uncertain about their future role in the industry. Contracts for oil supplies were increasingly being negotiated between the governments of consuming and producing countries. France, for example, signed a long-term deal with Saudi Arabia and Britain had agreed a contract with Iran. The oil companies, it seemed, were in danger of being squeezed out of existence, or at least of having their roles greatly diminished. The answer, obviously, was to diversify.

Like its competitors, BP set out to strengthen its downstream operations and make them profitable, and to diversify into alternative sources of energy and other industries where its experience looked relevant. This was more easily said than done.

Before 1973, oil had been a relatively cheap source of energy. As a result, oil consumption had increased rapidly, on average about one-and-a-half times as fast as the general rate of economic growth in the industrialized countries. After 1973, oil was no longer cheap and oil consumption fell faster than the general decline in economic activity. In 1976, the economies of the industrial countries began to recover, but oil remained expensive and consumers tried to use as little as possible. So oil consumption rose more slowly than overall economic growth. This left the oil companies burdened with surplus refining and shipping capacity which had been built up before 1973 on the false assumption that rapid growth in oil use would continue.

As a result, BP's downstream business had deep problems. The group's worldwide sales of oil products remained below 1973's level for four years after the price shock. They were higher in 1978 thanks only to growth in the USA. In Europe, BP's sales were still less than they had been five years earlier.

The company's first reaction to the problem of surplus refining capacity in Europe came in 1973, when it sold its marketing network and refining interests in Italy to a consortium organized by the Monti group. Five

A geologist examines core
samples at the Olympic Dam
mine in South Australia. BP
sold its 49-per-cent interest in
the mine in 1993.

Sir David Steel, chairman
from 1975 to 1981, joined BP
in 1950 after early success
in the legal profession.
His chairmanship saw
the development and
commissioning of the Prudhoe
Bay field in Alaska and major
investment in the North Sea.

Possibly the most successful
promotional campaign ever run
by BP, the Smurfs rapidly
became collectors' items for
adults and children alike.

years later it acted more aggressively, purchasing refining and marketing assets as well as gas and coal interests from the Veba group in Germany. These included a 25-per-cent stake in Ruhrgas, the second largest gas distributor in Europe after British Gas. As the capacity of the refining plant owned by Veba was smaller than the volume of its sales, the take-over increased the utilization of Deutsche BP's own refineries.

BP's downstream operations in the UK were transformed in the mid-1970s by the dissolution of the long-standing partnership with Shell. BP had always chafed at being the junior partner. In future BP Oil (later BP Oil UK) would handle all the group's supply, refining, distribution and marketing operations in the UK.

The break-up of Shell-Mex and BP was far from simple and there was some spirited bargaining over market shares. The actual split in the UK took place on New Year's Day 1976, but this was only the beginning. One of the absolute points of agreement between Shell and BP was the importance of calculating their individual bills to their newly respective customers exactly. The tiniest error would be enough excuse to delay a payment for at least a month. To everyone's satisfaction, the new systems operated almost perfectly.

Most British consumers remained unaware of the separation. But signs that independence was spurring BP's marketing efforts began to show with the arrival in the UK of the Smurfs in 1978. These little blue creatures in Phrygian caps, the invention of Belgian cartoonist Pierre Culliford, had been a runaway success for BP throughout Europe since 1969. The initial reaction of Eric Daykin, National Benzole's sales director, to the idea of using Smurfs to sell his brand in Britain, however, was 'Ugh!' Their success was almost embarrassing. 'I would stress that Smurfs were introduced purely to gild cash tills, not to boost gallonage, which would have been utterly incompatible with the need to conserve fuel,' Daykin piously told BP's staff magazine, *Shield*.

BP and Shell also split their marketing operations in the parts of Africa and the Middle East which had been covered by the Consolidated Petroleum Company. The most important single market in the Consolidated area was South Africa, where BP and Shell separated their operations in June 1975. Not long afterwards, allegations were made in the world press that Shell and BP had been supplying fuel from South Africa to Ian Smith's rebel government in Southern Rhodesia in spite of trade sanctions. In 1977 David Owen, Foreign Secretary in Harold Wilson's government, appointed Queen's Counsel Thomas Bingham to investigate the matter. Bingham estimated that about 13 million barrels of oil had been supplied to Rhodesia from orders placed with Shell and BP in South Africa since 1966. BP's discomfited management took measures to prevent the acceptance of orders for oil destined for Rhodesia, but too late to prevent damage to the company's reputation.

BP also had problems on the shipping side. Like the rest of the industry, it had embarked on a crash programme to increase shipping capacity after the Six Day War closed the Suez Canal. New supertankers continued to roll inexorably off Japanese production lines long after sales, especially of crude oil, fell back after the 1973 oil crisis. Yet the company's need for ships also fell as output increased from the North Sea. As a result, BP found itself with a chronic excess of tanker tonnage. One opportunity to reduce the size of the fleet was seized in 1976 when David Steel signed an agreement with Dr Manuchehr Eghbal, chairman of the National Iranian Oil Company, to form the Irano-British Shipping Company. Iran bought three large modern tankers and two smaller product carriers from the BP Tanker Company (formerly the British Tanker Company), which supplied five matching vessels to the joint venture.

The jointly owned South African subsidiaries of Shell and BP were criticized in the Bingham Report for breaking UN sanctions by supplying oil to the illegal government in Rhodesia, headed by Ian Smith (above).

Left During the mid-1970s, BP invested heavily in coal. The picture shows miners at the Ermelo coalmine in South Africa in 1979.

A worker at the Old Ben 1 coalmine in Illinois, USA, in 1987. In that year, BP acquired the Old Ben Coal Company as part of its take-over of Standard Oil's portfolio of assets.

Polyethylene granules and
pipes manufactured from BP
Chemicals' linear low-density
polyethylene.

Other measures to reduce the shipping surplus included scrapping smaller, less efficient vessels, laying up many new tankers and reducing the speed of crude carriers to increase the stocks of oil held in the floating supply line. By the end of 1978 the number of ships operated by BP had fallen to 115. Six years earlier it had been 311.

But as fast as BP and other oil companies reduced their shipping fleets, they expanded in new directions as they rushed to diversify into other industries. Some diversifications were bizarre. Mobil even bought Barnum and Bailey's Circus. Most, however, chose to invest in other extractive and energy industries.

The decision to invest in coal was made on the assumption that the price of solid fuel must inevitably be driven up to the calorific equivalent of oil. BP was impressed by a long-term estimate that the energy coefficient of the world's recoverable coal reserves was 11 times the total for oil and gas. This looked an infallible combination. BP Coal was formed in March 1974 and within three years the group had bought a 50-per-cent share in the Clutha mine in New South Wales, Australia's second largest coal exporter, for £115m. and committed itself to spending an extra £35m. on improvements over the next decade. In Canada, another £17m. was invested in coal licences in north-eastern British Columbia, where BP was contemplating spending £100m. more on development. A further £22m. was put into a coalmine in South Africa. BP also began exploring for coal elsewhere in Australia, Canada and southern Africa, as well as Indonesia and Colombia. By 1985 the company hoped to be producing 20 million tons a year. Prospects already looked good by 1977, with the price of coking coal double the level three years earlier.

BP began to invest in other minerals as well. Its portfolio was given a big boost in 1980 by the acquisition of Selection Trust, a London-based company with mineral interests in Australia, the USA, Canada, and Africa. The board took the view that nuclear power was too vulnerable to political and environmental hazards. But that did not stop the company searching for uranium as well as other metals around the world and joining a consortium investigating deep-sea mining in the Pacific. At the same time,

BP Chemicals' acrylonitrile
plant at Lima, Ohio, USA.
Ninety-five per cent of the
world's acrylonitrile
manufacturing capacity uses
BP technology under licence.

Left From being a simple poultry-feed supplier, BP Nutrition developed over the years to become a world-class animal-feed producer and also a supplier of poultry and pig-breeding stock.

As well as feeding animals, BP Nutrition maintained a very successful business supplying high-quality *charcuterie* to customers throughout Europe.

it expanded its chemicals interests. BP built new manufacturing plants for acetic acid, benzene, polythene, polypropylene, polystyrene and PVC in the UK, France and Germany, as well as an ethylene cracker on Teesside in the north of England, in partnership with ICI. Acquisitions from Monsanto and Union Carbide in Europe further enlarged the business and by 1979 sales of chemical products totalled 4.5 million tons.

The company was also building up its nutrition business. In 1971 BP Proteins had formed a joint company with ANIC, part of the Italian state oil corporation, ENI. By 1976 a plant capable of producing 100,000 tons a year of an oil-derived protein named Toprina had been built in Sardinia. But then the use of Toprina in animal feedstuffs was banned by the Italian authorities, even though they had approved it four years earlier.

BP Nutrition, as BP Proteins was renamed, had already begun to purchase animal-feed companies as outlets for Toprina. Cooper Nutrition Products was bought in 1975, followed by Dutch animal-feed company Trouw. Although plans to produce Toprina had to be abandoned, BP stayed in the animal-feed business. BP Nutrition expanded rapidly, acquiring the animal-feed firms of Hendrix, Skretting, Nanta and Noria. In 1986, BP Nutrition bought Purina Mills, making the group the biggest supplier of animal feed in the USA. 'A glass of champagne to celebrate another deal was something of a frequent occurrence,' said Eddie Brouwer, then BP Nutrition's managing director. BP also retained its computer subsidiary, Scicon.

The change from an integrated oil business into a diversified multi-industry group put pressure on BP's management structure. A detailed organization study was started in 1977 and a new structure put in place in 1981. It took a form then fashionable in large organizations: a management matrix.

BP's matrix was made up of a warp of international businesses and a weft of national associates. Initially there were nine international

In the 1960s, BP acquired a computer services company, CEIR, which changed its name to Scientific Control Systems (Scicon) in 1968.

116 Diversification led BP into the development of advanced materials for the aerospace industry on both sides of the Atlantic. In California, a production supervisor checks the highly sophisticated composite domes used to cover the radar systems of military command planes.

Until the divestment of its detergents interests in 1993, BP had produced detergents from derivatives of oil and chemicals for more than 30 years. During the 1980s, BP achieved a prominent position for its private-label personal-care and household products not only in Singapore, as seen here, but in markets throughout the world.

businesses: oil exploration and production; oil refining and marketing; chemicals; minerals; gas; coal; nutrition; detergents; and new ventures. Two more, computer systems and shipping, were added later. These were interwoven with 70 national associates, from BP Australia to BP Zimbabwe, which ran group business activities at country level.

The idea was to balance the responsibilities of the national associates and the international businesses. It was admitted at the time that it was a complicated structure, but one reflecting the complexity of BP's geographical and functional diversity. This, however, had not been simplified by dramatic new developments in the Middle East.

At the end of the 1970s the world was rocked by another oil shock comparable to that of 1973. Signs that the Shah was losing his grip on his turbulent country were becoming more and more alarming. Support for the exiled Shi'ite ayatollah, Ruhollah Khomeini, had escalated into demonstrations and riots since an article attacking him had been published in a Tehran newspaper in January 1978. By August the unrest had reached the oil industry. In October striking workers moved into the offices of the Oil Service Company, the descendant of Iranian Oil Participants and largely staffed by expatriate oilmen. Within a month Iran's exports had fallen from four-and-a-half million barrels a day to less than a million. By Christmas, all exports of Iranian oil had ceased. Three weeks later, the Shah boarded a plane at Tehran airport and left his country for ever.

Other Middle Eastern countries hurried to raise their output, and supplies to the rest of the world fell by only about two million barrels a day during the first quarter of 1979, a reduction of approximately 4 per cent in actual consumption. The effect on the market should not have been dramatic. But panic seized the world's consumers of oil. Just as in 1973, buyers everywhere rushed to build up stocks – the companies to hold their market shares and meet their contractual obligations, major users in industry and power generation to maintain output, domestic consumers to heat their houses and run their cars. There was only one outcome to this universal stockpiling – a drastic shortage of day-to-day supplies out of all proportion to the actual reduction in world oil supplies. The result was a crisis at the pumps and a wild leap in the spot price of oil.

BP, a large purchaser of Iranian oil, was badly affected by the loss of supplies. Its position was worsened by events in Nigeria, where BP had been lifting about 250,000 barrels a day of equity crude. On 31 July 1979 Nigeria's military government, headed by General Obasanjo, informed BP that its interests were to be taken over by the state with effect from midnight. Nigerian officials told BP representatives in Lagos that the action was in direct response to the policy of Margaret Thatcher's Conservative government, which it was claimed had 'positively encouraged' BP to sell oil to South Africa. They argued that because of the large UK-government shareholding, BP was not a free agent and could be forced to supply oil to South Africa. Despite Nigerian denials, the nationalization was seen as an attempt to influence Britain's policy towards Zimbabwe, the new name for Rhodesia, which was to be discussed at a forthcoming meeting of Commonwealth heads of government in Zambia. For its part, BP felt it was being used as a political football.

Altogether, as a result of events in Iran and Nigeria, BP's direct supplies of oil dropped by about three million barrels a day. The company declared *force majeure* on its long-term contracts, but this still left it needing another two million barrels a day to maintain supplies to its UK and European refineries. Finding this oil in the open market at anything like reasonable prices tested BP's trading team to the limit. When Sir David Steel told *Shield*, 'The people who used to sell our oil have suddenly had to become pretty expert at buying it,' it was something of an understatement.

However, new supplies of oil from the North Sea and Alaska, and the stockpiles of Iranian and Nigerian oil held along its lengthy supply line, insulated BP from serious damage. In fact, 1979 turned out to be the company's most profitable year so far, with net profits up from £444m. to £1,620m. As in 1974, these exceptional earnings were largely attributable to 'paper' profits made on the oil stocks BP was holding. But that did not stop the directors raising the dividend from less than 6.5p per share to nearly 20p per share. Although the chairman warned that the company's long-term position depended on the health of world trade, the general feeling was that BP had snatched something close to triumph from the jaws of catastrophe.

General Obasanjo, leader of Nigeria's military government, nationalized BP's interests in the country overnight on 31 July 1979.

117

In remote parts of the world without access to mains electricity, power produced by BP Solar's panels provides vital energy for lighting, refrigeration and heating.

Chapter Fifteen

No Sacred Cows

Left Standard Oil of Ohio (Sohio) was the original Standard Oil founded by entrepreneur and philanthropist John D Rockefeller in Cleveland in 1870. BP acquired a 25-per-cent interest in Sohio in 1970, and progressively built up its holding. In 1987, Sohio was bought outright by BP and merged with the group's other interests in the USA to form a new company, BP America.

The euphoria did not take long to wear off. Fears of oil shortages revived in September 1980 when Saddam Hussein launched Iraq's armed forces against Iran, once again depriving the world of a large helping of Middle Eastern oil. Spot prices for oil soared to $42 a barrel.

For a brief period inflated oil prices buoyed up BP's results in spite of heavy 'windfall' taxes. A special supplementary petroleum duty of £500m. boosted taxes and royalties from BP's North Sea oil and gas income to £2.4 billion in 1981, equal to a quarter of Britain's total Public Sector Borrowing Requirement that year. But again the high price of oil was driving energy consumption down and the industrial nations of the world into recession. BP might be making large profits from its new North Sea and Alaskan oil, but all its other businesses were in big trouble. In the winter of 1981–2, BP's European refining and marketing operations were losing £1m. a day and petrochemicals another £500,000.

Peter Walters was chosen to succeed Sir David Steel as chairman at the relatively young age of 49 with a specific brief to tackle the crisis. His appointment in 1981 coincided with the board's conclusion that the fall in demand for oil products was not a blip. Refining, marketing, shipping and petrochemicals, BP's forecasters predicted, were all facing a bleak future in which margins would become ever tighter. They saw this as especially true in Europe, where the bulk of the company's downstream investments was concentrated.

Right Sir Peter Walters, BP's chairman from 1981 to 1990, on a visit to Egypt in 1981. He was appointed to the BP board in February 1973. His decade at the helm included the momentous year of 1987, when BP fully took over Standard Oil and began the Britoil acquisition, and the UK government sold its remaining shares in the company.

120 BP's ethylene and ethane activities in the UK in the early 1980s were concentrated at Grangemouth, Scotland, where the use of North Sea gas as a feedstock gave the plant a competitive edge.

During a lull in fighting in the 1980-8 Iran-Iraq war, Iranian troops perch on the top of their tank, adorned with a poster of Ayatollah Khomeini. The war, which prevented much Middle East oil from reaching world markets, caused prices to soar to $42 a barrel.

The key change in BP's management structure, prepared to coincide with Walter's appointment as chairman, was the setting up of the matrix which counterbalanced national companies with international business streams. This was to set the tone for BP's structure for the next two decades. Among the senior executives chosen to lead the new streams were Robert Horton and David Simon. Horton was put in charge of petrochemicals; Simon was made responsible for downstream oil.

Walters decided that the first oil group to slash its capacity in all these areas would benefit most. He made two assumptions. One was that there was so much surplus capacity that, for the foreseeable future at least, BP would always be able to buy supplies or services cheaply. The other was that the first company to act would be the only one to achieve large-scale closures and redundancies without being blocked by socialist governments or powerful trades unions. 'I saw it was very obvious what we had to do in terms of cash containment, cash limits on spending,' Walters said. 'And we'd got two years to do it.'

He also appreciated the need to sell the cuts internally. 'I think any general has to have some catchphrases, at the risk of their becoming platitudes. Part of my message was that there were no sacred cows in BP. It was simple to say, "No sacred cows", but it released a lot of people's inhibitions about suggesting, for example, "We ought to close the Kent refinery but there are two thousand people there."'

The other part of the new chairman's message was that BP's traditional strategy of being big was irrelevant if divorced from profitability. 'In our coal business we had said that it was our aim to have 20 million tons of producible coal by 1985. I said I didn't care if we were selling one million or 100 million tons, as long as every step was profitable.'

He began by slashing refining capacity. In three years BP took 300m.

barrels out of its European operations by closing nine refineries, three each in the UK, France and Germany, leaving it with one in each country. In Britain the survivor was Grangemouth, nearest to BP's North Sea oilfields.

Then the company stripped its chemicals activities right down to core businesses. 'We concentrated in the UK on making ethylene and ethane at Grangemouth, where North Sea gas gave us a competitive edge, acetic acids and nitriles, where we were the market leader, and polyethylene, using the low-pressure gas phase process that we had developed at Lavéra and licensed around the world,' said Walters. The rest of the chemicals division was ruthlessly disposed of in whatever way was possible. For example, Walters and Horton negotiated a swap of BP's PVC interests for ICI's low-density polyethylene business.

Next came shipping. Following the cutbacks in the mid-1970s, this division had changed its name in 1980 to BP Shipping, reflecting an attempt to find other cargoes such as coal and liquid gas. But it had remained a high-cost company. Almost all its staff were BP employees, from the most junior ratings up. As the sector was depressed by an awesome quantity of surplus tonnage this tradition was under pressure, especially as Walters was insisting that BP Shipping, too, become a profit centre. In 1984 the company launched a sales drive aimed at maximizing the return on BP's fleet of high-technology vessels, mainly used to support offshore oilfields. It also began searching for new bulk cargoes for its coastal carriers and large tankers.

Hopes that a 'premium quality' shipping company could compete were soon dashed. Both the bulk and the offshore markets collapsed and by the end of 1985 BP Shipping had accumulated losses of £160m. In January 1986 the company handed over all its vessels to independent manning agencies. BP's 1,690 sea-going staff were then given the choice of

121

A NASA Boeing 747 carrying the prototype space shuttle, *Enterprise*, is fuelled by Air BP at Stansted Airport, England, in 1983.

BP tankers at BP's busy Rotterdam refinery in the Netherlands, 1980.

Since its inception in 1982, BP's Wytch Farm onshore oilfield in southern England has won many awards for environmental management. The picture shows 'nodding donkeys' in October 1984 when production averaged 4,000 barrels of oil a day. The oilfield now produces 95,000 barrels a day.

working directly for the new agents or taking redundancy payments or early retirement.

Walters paid equal attention to restoring BP's finances. 'We deliberately built up a £2-billion war-chest. We were lucky. We had the revenues coming in from Alaska and the North Sea and we were able to take the cost of the closures and build up capital for subsequent redeployment.' The cash build-up was boosted by a mammoth rights issue in 1981 which raised £624m. – and incidentally further diluted the government's shareholding, as the Treasury declined the opportunity to take up its rights. Towards the end of 1983 BP raised another £292m. by selling 11 per cent of the Forties field to 21 other companies.

Having sorted out the European businesses, BP turned its attention to its North American investments. On the surface, these were doing well. In Alaska a new oilfield named Kuparuk, in which BP owned 29 per cent and Sohio another 9 per cent, had come on stream in December 1981. Kuparuk, about 30 miles west of Prudhoe Bay, contained an estimated four billion barrels of oil. It had cost $3 billion to develop, but financing it was no problem. Sohio, with its share of Prudhoe Bay's output, was awash with cash which its board had hastened to invest elsewhere. Since 1977 Sohio had acquired exploration rights over nearly four million acres, some offshore in the Gulf of Mexico and others outside the USA, but most in southern states such as Arkansas, Oklahoma and Texas, where it was spending lavishly. BP's own geologists were unimpressed by the oil potential of much of this 'cow pasture'.

Driven by the same gloomy assumptions about prospects for oil that

had influenced BP, Sohio also invested extravagantly in minerals. It went into coal in a big way and, in June 1981, took over Kennecott Corporation, the largest copper producer in the USA, for $1.7 billion. Kennecott produced 300,000 tons of copper as well as gold, silver, molybdenum and other minerals. It had mining and manufacturing interests in 21 US states and 21 foreign countries, and its assets were valued at $3 billion. But within months John Miller, Sohio's president, was having to defend the take-over. Low mineral prices meant Kennecott had lost money ever since its acquisition. So, unhappily, had many of Sohio's other purchases. Altogether, BP calculated that Sohio had sunk $6 billion of its Alaskan revenues in unprofitable investments in the USA.

BP's original agreement with Sohio had pledged it not to interfere in the management of the US group. In any case, the arguments that Sohio was deploying to justify its diversifications were the same as those BP was using for its own investments in coal and minerals. But by 1986 Sir Peter Walters had decided BP could no longer stand by and watch. Alton Whitehouse, the chairman of Sohio – or Standard Oil, as it had just renamed itself, all the other fragments of John D Rockefeller's dismembered cartel having either changed their names or disappeared – was on BP's main board. Walters called him into his office after a regular Thursday morning meeting and passed him a letter. It summarized Standard Oil's recent appalling record and called for the resignations of Whitehouse and Miller. In their place Robert Horton was proposed as chief executive and John Browne, BP's young head of finance, as chief financial officer.

'Al, this letter will be hand-delivered to each of your non-executive directors in the States in an hour's time,' Walters explained. 'I will be in

The Bingham Canyon mine in Utah, USA, part of the Kennecott assets which were taken over by Standard Oil in 1981 and later passed to BP. Bingham Canyon is the world's biggest open-cast copper mine.

Before its take-over by BP, Standard Oil had invested heavily in coal and minerals companies, such as QIT Minerals in Canada. The picture shows the high-purity iron-casting operation at the QIT plant in Quebec.

A production platform in BP's Beatrice oilfield in the Moray Firth, Scotland. Beatrice, formerly jointly owned with Britoil, became wholly owned by BP after its successful bid for that company in 1987.

Britoil

Cleveland tomorrow morning with my deputy chairman, Roger Bexon, and I want you to assemble all your executive directors and we will tell them what we are going to do.'

The problems facing Standard Oil's new management team were formidable. Prompt action was essential. Radical changes put in motion included disposing of many of Standard Oil's non-oil investments. A year later BP made a $7.6 billion offer for the 45 per cent of Standard Oil's shares it did not own. At the end of July 1987 Standard Oil was merged with BP's other US interests. With 43,000 employees and assets valued at $23 billion, BP America Inc. was the 13th largest industrial corporation in the USA, as well as the country's largest oil producer.

BP rounded off a momentous year by grabbing a 15-per-cent share stake in Britoil in a dawn raid on the London stock market and then launching a £2.5-billion offer for the whole of the company.

Britoil was the successor to the British National Oil Company, which Thatcher's government had privatized in 1982, retaining a 'golden share' giving it a majority vote at general meetings in certain circumstances. Since its formation in 1976, BNOC had received a 50-per-cent share of all new exploration concessions in the North Sea. By the time it was privatized, its rights extended over approximately 8,000 sq. km., about the same area held by BP. The two companies had joint interests in several oilfields, including Ninian, as well as a big new gas discovery called Bruce. Britoil's North Sea production was 170,000 barrels of oil and 240 million cu. ft of gas a day. Ownership of Britoil would add 40 per cent to BP's North Sea oil and gas reserves.

BP offered £5 for each Britoil share, against a market price early in December of £1.87. By the end of February the bid had succeeded. It was the first time that BP had bought oil reserves through the stock market, rather than developing them itself. Because the two companies were so close to each other on many of their concessions, it was a special case. The success of the Britoil bid cheered BP's directors. But they were still wondering what to do about a much bigger stock-market adventure earlier in 1987 which had ended up as a debacle.

Walters had been summoned to the Treasury in the autumn of 1986 to be told that the government intended to dispose of its remaining shareholding in BP. Although this was by then down to 32 per cent, the sell-off was likely to have a major influence on the company's share price.

'It is an enormous number of shares to put on the market,' the chairman remarked, 'the biggest private share sale the Stock Exchange has ever seen. I assume you plan to sell your holding in, say, three equal instalments over three years.' To his concern the reply was 'No'. So many privatization issues were in progress that the government had decided to put all its efforts to sell its BP shares into one marketing campaign, although payment by the new shareholders would be in three tranches.

Walters was unhappy, but BP had no choice except to co-operate. As the date for the announcement of the sale price drew near, the chairman and Robert Horton between them toured seven US cities in six days, making presentations to investment analysts and institutional investors. David Simon, the managing director handling BP's side of the share sale with the help of Rodney Chase, who had succeeded Browne as head of BP Finance, tackled the same task across Europe. Another managing director, Patrick Gillam, flew round the financial centres in the Far East on a similar mission.

On Thursday 15 October 1987, Walters watched Royal Marines abseil down the face of Britannic House as he stood beside Norman Lamont, Financial Secretary to the Treasury, who unveiled an offer price of 330p a share. That night a great storm struck the south-east of England. Only with hindsight did BP's chairman see it as an omen. The London stock market collapsed on the following 'Black' Monday and, four days later, the sale of the government's shares and the associated issue of new BP shares flopped horribly. BP had recommended that the secondary issue of new equity capital be withdrawn as there was clearly a very disturbed market for a sale of that size. The proposal was not accepted but a compromise safety-net solution for the Bank of England to purchase spare stock was rapidly formulated.

Walters also warned the Chancellor of the Exchequer, Nigel Lawson, that there was a risk that a large block of shares could fall into hostile

The strong American influence in this UK press advertisement for BP's 1987 annual report reflected the importance to the company of the acquisition of Standard Oil during that year.

125

During the late 1980s, the focus of BP's advertising turned from press to television. BP Oil developed a series of commercials which were scripted to allow them to be shown worldwide with the minimum of alteration for local markets. One of the most memorable campaigns showed an 'armada' of trucks, trains and planes bearing down on a startled motorist at a BP service station.

The British government's sale of its shares in BP in October 1987 should have been another triumph in its programme of privatization. Instead, the sale fell victim to Black Monday's panic in the world's stock markets, when more than £50 billion was wiped off share values in London. BP shares dropped well below the 330p offer price. The *Daily Express* report repeats the often-used but inaccurate description of BP as Britain's 'state oil firm'.

Panning for gold at a BP Minerals' project in central Kalimantan, Indonesia, 1988.

hands. His prediction was swiftly fulfilled when the Kuwait Investment Office bought a third of the shares on offer, giving it 10 per cent of BP's equity. The British government advised the KIO that this was enough. Two days later the Kuwaiti stake was up to 15 per cent. Next day the total was 18 per cent. The Kuwaiti Ambassador and Ali Khalifa, the Gulf state's Finance Minister, were summoned to a meeting with Lawson, Britain's Foreign Secretary, Sir Geoffrey Howe, and its Energy Secretary, Cecil Parkinson. Khalifa was told bluntly that no further investment was acceptable. Two more days passed and the Kuwaiti stake reached 22 per cent. It was a blatant snub to the British authorities.

BP objected strongly. It informed the British government that Kuwait might seek representation on its board, which would give the oil state the opportunity to learn all the group's plans and influence its strategy. Kuwait, it argued, might soon be in a position to dictate BP's North Sea oil production or insist the company invested in expensive desulphurization plant to treat imported Kuwaiti oil. The holding was, in the board's opinion, almost large enough to constitute a controlling interest.

Spurred into action, the government referred Kuwait's holding to the Monopolies and Mergers Commission, which decided Kuwait should be required to reduce it to below 10 per cent. How to achieve this was a different question. Finding buyers prepared to pay Kuwait £2 billion-plus for 790 million shares proved impossible while stock markets were so depressed. BP's directors were determined to resolve the situation. Eventually in January 1989 BP itself bought more than half the shares held by Kuwait, cancelling them afterwards.

The cost of the buy-back was coincidentally covered by the sale of most of BP's mineral interests to RTZ for £2.4 billion. 'I don't know whether we lost money on minerals overall,' Walters said later. 'We certainly paid far too much for the Australian venture. And there were new investments needed on a scale which we did not have the expertise to carry forward. Refocusing BP's asset base was already a strategic priority.'

BP Coal was also sold in 1989. BP had stayed behind this diversification for more than a decade but the endless competition between producers that persistently eroded margins had finally dispelled the company's belief in the potential of coal as a profit centre.

Sir Peter Walters wrote his last letter to BP shareholders in February 1990. He was able to report that the company had ended the 1980s with a record profit of more than £1.7 billion. Oil prices had recovered and demand was strong, thanks to the continuing economic boom. 'BP is now in a period of what could be termed aggressive consolidation,' he wrote. 'Our capital expenditure programme is focused on opportunities in our mainstream businesses: exploration and production, refining and marketing, and chemicals. Thus we are concentrating on our traditional areas of strength.' Although, he hastened to add, not so as to overlook BP's other investments in nutrition, research and technology, engineering and financial trading.

BP Exploration had raised over £300m. by selling royalty interests in Prudhoe Bay. The company planned to search for oil in new 'frontier' geological basins around the world, as well as continuing to exploit its existing oil and gas interests.

After 30 years, the familiar 'shield' logo had been redesigned to a style that would soon become recognized throughout the world. BP Oil had begun a three-year 'reimaging' programme to revamp the design of its 22,000 retail outlets and put them all under the single BP brand name. All its European operations had been grouped together as BP Oil Europe and it was looking hard at opportunities in eastern Europe.

BP Chemicals had made a record operating profit, although margins were once again coming under pressure. It planned to double ethylene production at Grangemouth.

The group had committed itself to further safety and anti-pollution efforts, following the *Exxon Valdez* catastrophe in Alaska.

'Robert Horton succeeds me as chairman on 11 March and David Simon becomes deputy chairman. I am confident I am passing on a company in excellent shape for the busy and promising future ahead,' Walters told BP's shareholders.

127

The first service station to be converted to BP's new livery was at Stoke Newington, London, in 1990. Over the next three years, the entire worldwide network was 'reimaged'.

BP Chemicals' ethylene cracker at Baglan Bay, south Wales, opened in 1972. Industry over-capacity forced its closure in 1994, and its production now concentrates on vinyl acetate monomer, isopropanol, ethanol and styrene.

Chapter Sixteen

BP United

Left Employee at BP Oil's Alliance refinery near New Orleans, one of BP's three refineries in the USA. During 1994, a $100-million upgrading project reinforced Alliance's position as one of the world's top-performing refineries.

Robert Horton was appointed chairman and chief executive of BP on his record. He had had an outstanding career in the group, successfully overseeing the rationalization programmes for shipping, chemicals and Standard Oil. He had scored a particular triumph in the USA, thanks to his dynamic, larger-than-life approach. Horton had handed over the job of chief executive of BP America early in 1988. Back in London, he had been given the job of overhauling the group's management structure.

The matrix system adopted at the beginning of the 1980s was no longer appropriate. The board's new strategy of concentrating on core businesses had reduced the number of international businesses to four. At the same time the geographic spread of BP's activities had begun to be seen in regional rather than national terms. The matrix structure also relied on a 'command and control' basis which was felt to be outdated.

Right The *British Tamar* moors beside the Queen Elizabeth II bridge on the River Thames at Dartford, near London, en route to BP Oil's massive terminal at Grangemouth in Scotland, 1994.

In the course of revitalizing Standard Oil, Horton had encouraged much greater delegation of responsibility to the individual and what he described as 'leaner, looser, styles of management control'. He had also been converted to a belief in the potential of information technology for reducing hierarchies and bureaucracy.

It was these radical American influences that dominated 'Project 1990', the title Horton gave to his proposals for reorganizing BP as a whole. They were a mixture of the practical and the aspirational. The practical included eliminating layers of management and sharply reducing staff at the group's London headquarters to the point where the 32-storey skyscraper became surplus to requirements. The surviving staff, a mere 350 compared with more than 2,000 under Walters, moved back into the Lutyens-designed

Robert Horton joined BP in 1957. In the 1980s he played a central role in reshaping BP Chemicals and Standard Oil. Horton was BP chairman and chief executive officer from 1990 to 1992.

Lord Ashburton, formerly Sir John Baring, became a non-executive director of BP in 1982. After the resignation of Robert Horton in June 1992, the roles of chairman and chief executive were separated. Lord Ashburton became chairman, while the role of group chief executive was taken by David Simon.

office block on Finsbury Circus, built for Anglo-Persian in the 1920s, although behind its original neo-classical façade the interior had been almost totally rebuilt.

Horton regretted the job losses but saw them as an essential precursor to the aspirational phase, in which he planned to change BP's whole culture. Horton had a vision. He was going to make BP 'the most successful oil company of the 1990s and beyond'. He set out to persuade everyone in the company to subscribe to it.

The new chairman introduced 'culture change' workshops for senior managers. Throughout BP, employees began to feel the effect of his demand that they take greater personal responsibility for improving their contribution. The new approach, with its greater openness, fewer committees and more personal accountability, was welcomed by many. But it was certainly unsettling to the prevailing ethos within the company.

Horton believed that individual 'empowerment' would increase BP's ability to 'manage surprise'. His faith was swiftly to be tested. Surprises abounded, beginning with the invasion of Kuwait by Saddam Hussein's army at the beginning of August 1990. Almost overnight spot prices for crude oil doubled from around $15 a barrel to more than $30. As BP had no significant contracts with either Iraq or Kuwait, its oil supplies were not directly affected.

In military terms, the Gulf crisis lasted for six months, culminating in the Allied invasion of Iraq in the early hours of 17 January 1991. When the initial air strike was reported, the spot price for oil bounded to $40 a barrel. But within hours, as news of the Allies' dramatic success filtered back, the price collapsed, falling to $20 a barrel. With the threat that Hussein might destroy Saudi Arabian production removed, the danger of further reductions in Middle Eastern oil exports was clearly over.

As a result, oil prices were free to reflect the deepening recession that was undermining demand for energy throughout the industrialized world. BP was badly hit on all fronts. Margins on its North Sea and Alaskan crude oil production contracted and its profits from oil refining and marketing were squeezed as sales revenues dropped and competition intensified. The group's other activities, in particular chemicals, suffered severely too. Low economic growth rates in the UK and industry-wide overcapacity were at the root of the cyclical downturn.

All this was leading to a growing stock-market disenchantment with BP and its prospects. This sentiment was not helped when, early in 1992, Robert Horton announced a 14-per-cent decline in the group's profits. Nonetheless, he said the board was still convinced that BP's strategy remained sound and that, despite the reduction in profits, he was committed to maintaining dividends as well as capital investment because he was confident oil prices would revive. His belief that BP should continue to spend its way through the recession was badly received by some institutional investors, who were concerned about the company's high level of debt. There were rumours, too, of a boardroom rift, which BP resolutely denied. Far from recovering, the share price fell further.

In the two years that he had been in the chair, Horton had acquired a high profile outside BP. His status as the head of one of Britain's largest companies ensured that his statements on matters such as an expected recovery in the oil price had been widely reported. Rightly or wrongly, the press, analysts and other commentators were increasingly taking an unfavourable view of BP and this, coming on top of the company's worsening results, was having a corrosive effect on staff morale. Deeply concerned, the non-executive directors conferred after a visit by the board to BP's Alaskan operations. Although they publicly supported the fundamental objectives being pursued by Horton, they reluctantly concluded that his management style had turned out not to be right for the company.

The board recognized, too, that although the changes Horton had initiated had produced remarkable improvements in many areas, the new corporate culture needed defining and consolidating. This could only be done by somebody else. Horton, the non-executive directors agreed sombrely, was not a credible brakeman for his own revolution.

Horton's departure on 25 June 1992 was traumatic for everyone connected with BP. There was no disguising that it reflected a major management crisis. The directors hastened to assure shareholders, employees and customers that the company was fundamentally sound and that all that was involved was a change of style.

The first step in rebuilding confidence was the immediate appointment of John Baring, the seventh Baron Ashburton, as non-executive chairman of BP. Lord Ashburton had been a non-executive director of BP since 1982, which made him the longest-serving member of the board. He had also spent 15 years as chairman of the merchant bank which for the previous 230 years had carried his family's name, retiring in 1990. 'I can't say that being chairman of BP was ever part of my game-plan,' he admitted. But he added that he was delighted to take on the job, even though the circumstances in which he did so were unhappy.

David Simon was made chief executive and remained deputy chairman. Although he and Horton were contemporaries, they had spent most of their careers in BP in different areas of the group. While Horton had been making his name in shipping, chemicals and the USA, Simon had built his reputation in European marketing. In the late 1970s he had been closely associated with BP's major reorganization into business streams and in 1982 had taken over as chief executive of BP Oil International, the group's downstream oil business. Afterwards, as group finance director, he had made a central contribution to the take-overs of Standard Oil and Britoil and to the resolution of the ill-fated government share sale. However, Simon had worked with Horton for two years, as they prepared the changes that Project 1990 introduced to BP, and was closely involved in their implementation.

In contrast with Horton's flamboyant, expansive style, Simon had a calmer, more intuitive approach. He said that BP's primary goal should be creating value for its shareholders. 'All our other aims – finding more oil or gas, getting it safely and profitably to the market, serving customers

Sir David Simon, knighted in June 1995, joined BP in 1961 and built his reputation in European marketing. A board member since 1986, he became group chief executive in 1992 and chairman in 1995.

BP Chemicals announced in 1995 an expansion of its KG (Kinneil Grangemouth) plant in Scotland to meet increased demand for ethylene. By 1996, the plant's total ethylene capacity will be 700,000 tons a year.

Air BP refuels a US Air Force F-14 fighter at the Ellington Base near Houston, Texas, in 1989. BP received praise from the US forces for its role in meeting the fuel requirements of the Allied forces during the Desert Shield and Desert Storm campaigns of the Gulf War.

In July 1995, John Browne was appointed chief executive of the BP group at the age of 47. After holding senior positions in BP Exploration, BP Finance and Standard Oil, in 1989 he became chief executive of BP Exploration. He was appointed to the BP board in 1991.

more effectively, protecting the environment – either lead to that central goal or, in the end, are impossible without it,' he stated.

Lord Ashburton explained the decision to split the functions of the chairman and chief executive in a letter to shareholders dated 6 August 1992, a few weeks after the boardroom shake-up. 'I shall be responsible for the conduct of the board and its deliberations, and will be close to the development of strategy,' he wrote. 'This will leave David Simon and his fellow managing directors free to concentrate on formulating strategy for the board to consider, and for the day-to-day business of the company.' He added that the board felt a much more conservative approach to capital spending and dividends was needed to strengthen BP's balance sheet. To this end, the board was halving the dividend.

When the full results for 1992 were published in February 1993, they made depressing reading for BP's shareholders. For the first time since its rescue by the government in 1914, the company had made a loss, although admittedly only after allowing for write-offs and provisions of nearly £900m. for closures and job losses.

Lord Ashburton promised BP's shareholders a return to profitability through successful teamwork, beginning at the top of the company. Behind this intentionally low-key statement, a vigorous campaign to restore BP's fortunes was already under way. The real value of Project 1990 was to be tested by the need to change the performance of the group fundamentally.

David Simon laid out the aims of BP's new management team within days of taking over as chief executive. He labelled its targets 'One-Two-Five'. This was code for reducing corporate debt by $1 billion a year, raising profits to $2 billion by 1995, and cutting capital spending to $5 billion. He coined a new motto for BP: 'Profitability, Reputation and Teamwork', the initials PRT ironically echoing those of the Petroleum Revenue Tax that BP knew so well in its North Sea operations. In place of 'cultural change', the new team talked more of 'margins' and 'fine-tuning'.

An insistence on teamwork and performance was to become the bedrock of BP's new management style.

By the end of 1993, progress towards the new targets was impressive. Nearly $3 billion had already been shaved off the group's debt; profits had recovered to more than $1.5 billion; and capital spending had been held well below $5 billion. BP had also raised $3 billion by selling assets that were not performing well enough or no longer fitted with its core strategy of concentrating on its hydrocarbon-related businesses. BP Nutrition, the board had earlier decided, fell into the latter category, and in 1992 BP had begun to look for buyers for the division's businesses.

'Success contains within it the seeds of challenge,' Simon warned. 'Once people know you can deliver, they expect you to go on delivering. So we can't afford to relax for a minute.' BP's principal assets had to be made to work harder and operating costs watched even more closely.

Nor were the company's employees immune from the effects of this leaner business environment. The sale of some of BP's operating units, including their staff, coupled with savings from new technology and from contracting out activities previously performed in-house, brought numbers of employees down to 60,000 by the end of 1994, half the 1989 total.

In his report to shareholders in March 1995, BP's chief executive was able to state that the company had already reached the financial targets it had set itself in the middle of 1992. But now he produced a new set: a 50-per-cent rise in annual replacement cost earnings to $3 billion; a reduction in corporate debt to $8 billion by 1996; and a 'disciplined' increase in capital expenditure to between $4 billion and $4.5 billion in 1995 to secure future growth.

The successful completion of the recovery stage and the company's rapid progress towards its demanding new targets prompted an adjustment to BP's leadership. Now that the new executive team had proved itself, the board decided to initiate the next stage of BP's medium-term business development.

At the end of 1994, BP announced that David Simon was to succeed Lord Ashburton as chairman in July 1995, when he would hand over as chief executive to John Browne. BP was at pains to emphasize the planned nature of this change at the top and the continuity of management that it represented. Lord Ashburton spoke of his satisfaction that the three years of transition which had been his aim had been achieved.

To outside observers, the reshuffle marked a new phase in BP's recovery strategy and reflected renewed self-confidence. Within the company, no one doubted the energy that 47-year-old John Browne would bring to the direction of the group's affairs.

Since he joined BP as a university apprentice in 1966, Browne's reputation for driving himself had become legendary. Dispatched to the USA to help Horton reorganize Standard Oil, he had been made chief executive of that company's exploration and production arm in 1987, as well as executive vice-president and chief financial officer of BP America. In 1989, he had returned to London to become chief executive of BP Exploration. Two

In the home, the office, the factory and even the circus, products made from BP Chemicals' raw materials are in daily use.

133

Construction of a pipeline in Papua New Guinea in 1990 to transport gas from the Hides field on Mount Tumbudu, about 400 miles north-west of the capital Port Moresby. The gas is mainly used to power a nearby gold mine.

Right New fields are still being developed in the North Sea. Here the 85,000-ton concrete gravity base for BP's Harding field floats in the construction dock at Hunterston in April 1995.

134

Below A drilling site in Colombia, July 1994. Colombia is an area of growing importance to BP. The company also has substantial gas reserves in the country.

Right BP has interests in 323 mainly deep-water blocks in the Gulf of Mexico, where new technology is allowing drilling to take place at unprecedented depths.

years later, at the age of 43, he had been appointed to BP's main board. Now he was to head the management team in charge of a much slimmer and inherently more profitable company than the one which had begun the 1990s.

BP's upstream activities were thriving, despite an oil price that every year seemed to be lower than it was the year before. BP Exploration's success in the face of this declining price for its principal product was a vindication of the strategy it had adopted some five years earlier, with Robert Horton's full support.

This had built on the company's immense existing strength in Alaska and the North Sea and focused exploration efforts on prospects in new areas such as Colombia, Vietnam, Azerbaijan, the Gulf of Mexico and the deep Atlantic waters to the west of Shetland. Some of these had become accessible to BP because of the freer political environment ushered in by the collapse of communism and the ending of the Cold War. The door to others had been opened by the development of deep-water and drilling

technology which only a few years earlier would have been in the realm of science fiction.

A concerted drive to contain costs and improve productivity, coupled with innovative profit-sharing arrangements with suppliers, allowed BP Exploration to state in 1995 that its net income per barrel was the highest of all the major international oil companies.

Not only that: BP was finding more oil and gas than it was producing and at half the cost – an effective answer to those concerned about the company's dependence on what they saw as its declining reserves in Alaska and the North Sea. Moreover, the new reserves that were being added in places as far apart as Latin America, Vietnam and Azerbaijan were giving BP Exploration's portfolio a geographical diversity and balance it at one time had lacked.

In the downstream oil sector, the refining industry had seen its margins fall steeply since 1991. BP Oil launched a company-wide campaign to drive down its costs and raise productivity. The success of these self-help measures meant that, despite a halving of refining margins over the last three years, BP Oil's operating profit in 1994 was only slightly lower than in 1991.

There had been vigorous efforts, too, to improve the quality of BP's worldwide network of service stations. The least profitable had been sold off or closed, leaving the network with only 15,700 sites at the beginning of 1995 compared with more than 20,000 at the start of 1990. But the average volume of products sold by the remaining stations, and their profitability, had risen materially.

BP was also taking advantage of new opportunities in Europe. In 1991, BP Oil had bought a Spanish company called Petromed, which owned the

In the USA and elsewhere, BP service stations have now become fuel-and-food emporiums. Freshly baked bread, muffins and pastries, gourmet coffees, fresh fruit and other high-quality products are available round the clock.

135

Baku, Azerbaijan, 1993. BP is a member of a consortium of Western oil companies which in 1994 signed a contract for the development of several large oilfields in the Caspian Sea. Oil seepages around Baku were noted as early as the 13th century.

Castellón refinery, one of the most modern in Europe, and held a 9-percent share of the Spanish retail petrol and diesel market. Now that the Iron Curtain was down, BP service stations were springing up in the Czech Republic, Hungary and eastern Germany, and plans were in place to open in Poland and Moscow.

Close attention was also being given to the Asia-Pacific region. Australia and New Zealand had long occupied an important place in BP's downstream portfolio, but a $240m. investment in its jointly owned refinery in Singapore, an expansion of its retail network in Malaysia and the dynamic growth of its lubricants business in Vietnam were all evidence of BP Oil's determination to strengthen its position in this high-growth area. BP Chemicals, too, which was already benefiting from a polyethylene plant in Indonesia and an acetyls plant in Korea, was planning more investment in these countries, as well as in Malaysia and China.

The early 1990s had not been kind to BP Chemicals, which had struggled against the effects of continuing recession in its main markets and chronic over-capacity in the petrochemicals industry. But, after three years

Above Eastern Europe is a market of growing importance to BP Oil. A BP service station stands in Muhlenstrasse, beside a short section of the former Berlin Wall, colourfully decorated by local graffiti artists.

Right The Castellón refinery in Spain, acquired by BP in 1991 as part of its purchase of Petromed, is sited on the coast near Valencia, at the heart of Spain's 'golden triangle' where 60 per cent of the country's oil consumption takes place.

Waste gas is flared as the drilling rig *Ocean Guardian* conducts an extended-well test in the Foinaven field, part of BP's new oil province west of Shetland in the deep waters of the Atlantic frontier. In the background is the *Sovereign Explorer*, one of four rigs drilling exploration and appraisal wells in the area in 1994.

Demand for energy is surging in the Asia-Pacific region. Here a BP tanker driver delivers fuel to a service station in Malaysia.

Environmental monitoring at the 200,000-tons-a-year acetic acid plant at Ulsan, South Korea, a joint venture between BP Chemicals and Korean corporation, Samsung.

of very poor results, 1994 and 1995 saw a strong resurgence in its profits, thanks to energetic self-help measures to cut costs, raise productivity and redefine its business portfolio, and a long-overdue firming of market prices.

For the new chief executive, John Browne, a key factor behind BP's improving business performance was the way it was exploiting the opportunities offered by new technology. At Sunbury, and at many other sites across the company, multi-disciplined teams were applying the latest technology to come up with solutions which cut the cost of projects and brought them more rapidly to the cash-generating stage.

As BP entered its 87th year, the mood in the company could best be described as confident. After a period when every plan, every action had been aimed at restoring the financial equilibrium temporarily lost in the early 1990s, BP was readying itself for a period of what its new chairman, Sir David Simon, called 'disciplined growth'. The company's better performance now offered a 'gateway' to that growth, he told BP's shareholders.

BP was a much changed organization. Gone were the old simplicities, when all that mattered was to find oil and build a pipeline. The modern BP was an integrated international oil company, its profitability coming as much from its success in providing high-quality service to its customers as from its skill at finding and extracting oil and gas from increasingly challenging environments.

To a large extent BP had returned to its roots. The company was once more concentrating on the business it knew best – the production and sale of hydrocarbons and their derivatives. William Knox D'Arcy would be amazed by the changes in the world since he had sought his original concession in Persia in 1901, but he would have no trouble recognizing the business that he founded.

It would be surprising, however, if he were not impressed by its achievements.

Index